Home Life
Pat Hodgson

Batsford Academic and Educational Ltd   London

© Pat Hodgson 1982
First published 1982
All rights reserved. No part of this publication may be reproduced, in any form or by any means, without permission from the publishers.

Typeset by DP Press, Sevenoaks
and printed in Great Britain by
R.J. Acford
Chichester, Sussex
for the publishers
Batsford Academic and Educational Ltd,
an imprint of B T Batsford Ltd,
4 Fitzhardinge Street,
London W1H 0AH

ISBN 0 7134 4085 6

ACKNOWLEDGMENT

The Author and Publishers would like to thank the following for their kind permission to reproduce copyright illustrations: Bodleian Library, Oxford, figs 14, 38, 40; BBC Hulton Picture Library, figs 8, 34, 51, 56, 57, 63; The British Library, fig 2; The Trustees of the British Museum, fig 54; Mel Calman, fig 64; Dover Publications, figs 7, 47; Greater London Council, figs 11, 32, 44; Imperial War Museum, figs 55, 58, 59; London Transport Board, fig 13; Museum of London, figs 20, 41, 43, 45; Punch, fig 33; Science Museum, London, figs 19, 24; Victoria and Albert Museum, figs 5, 22, 25, 30, 42, 50. Figs 1, 3, 4, 6, 9, 10, 15, 21, 23, 26, 27, 28, 29, 31, 36, 37, 39, 48, 49, 52, 53, 61, 62 are in the collection of the Author, who also did the picture research for the book.

Contents

Acknowledgment		2
List of Illustrations		4
1	Marriage and Children	5
2	A House to Live In	11
3	Home Comforts	19
4	Furnishings	29
5	Keeping House	36
6	The Consumer Society	50
7	A Classless Society	54
8	A Woman's Place	60
Biographies		66
Glossary		67
Note on old money and measures		68
Books for Further Reading		69
Museums		70
Index		71

List of Illustrations

1	A marriage contract	6
2	Fifteenth-century marriage	7
3	Engagement rings	8
4	Victorian wedding breakfast	9
5	Seventeenth-century family at home	9
6	Elizabethan cottage	11
7	Eighteenth-century cottage	12
8	Longleat House	13
9	"Jettied" houses	14
10	"Chambers"	15
11	"Back-to-back" housing	16
12	Peabody Square, Islington	16
13	Golders Green	17
14	Medieval open fire	19
15	A fireside seat	20
16	By the coal fire	21
17	A stand-pipe	22
18	Medieval baths	23
19	Victorian bath night	23
20	Elizabethan herb-burner	24
21	Privies	24
22	Candle-light	26
23	Paraffin lamp	26
24	Electrical appliances, 1894	27
25	Eighteenth-century wallpaper	28
26	Paint advertisement	28
27	Cottage interior	29
28	Fifteenth-century chair	30
29	Medieval chest	30
30	Eighteenth-century bedroom	32
31	A sideboard, 1903	32
32	A working-class home, 1911	33
33	A sitting room, 1930s	34
34	"Utility" furniture	34
35	Elizabethan maid	36
36	Vi-cocoa	37
37	Monkey Brand	38
38	Between-the-wars electrical appliances	39
39	Laundry maids	40
40	A mangle	40
41	The laundrette	41
42	Slaughtering the pig	42
43	Stewpot	43
44	A kitchen range	44
45	Pewter plate and tankards	45
46	Elizabethan family at table	46
47	A footman	47
48	Boot-cleaning	48
49	Victorian nursemaid	49
50	Pedlar dolls	50
51	Grocer's "boy"	51
52	Shoppers sculptures	52
53	*Home Companion* title page	52
54	Bovril	53
55	"Waste the Food and Help the Hun"	54
56	Council flats	56
57	Life on the dole	57
58	War economy dress	58
59	Evacuation Service poster	58
60	"Warm Thoughts about Matrimony"	60
61	Victorian mother and baby	62
62	Decorating the fireplace	63
63	Protest for nurseries	63
64	Calman cartoon	64

1
Marriage and Children

Arranged Marriages

Marriages everywhere, at any period of history, have one thing in common. They are a good excuse to have a party for relatives and friends. The wedding ceremony marks not only a new beginning for the happy couple, but also an alliance between two families. In the past the wishes of the families and the financial deals between them were of primary importance, and the feelings of the couple somewhat secondary. Rich landowners in the Middle Ages used their children like counters in a monopoly game to acquire money and estates. A marriage might also serve to strengthen a political alliance with another powerful family or bring in ready money when finances were low. Senior members of the two households got together to haggle over terms, and love did not really come into the picture. In some families children had little choice. When Elisabeth Paston refused to marry a widower of fifty in the fifteenth century, she was "beaten once in the week or twice, sometimes twice in one day, and her head broken in two or three places".

By the eighteenth century love matches were more common, although fathers still felt it their duty to provide a good marriage for their children. Squire Molesworth had to send his daughter to Ireland to find a husband that he could afford, saying: "We shall not have money enough to dispose of her here."

Marriage settlements were generally known and much discussed by family and friends. Lady Dysart thought her sister Fanny's marriage very suitable in 1748, because "he has £4000 a year in Scotland and two houses". In 1771 Parson Woodforde was much impressed with his cousin's wife, whom he considered "a very agreeable as well as handsome young Lady and has £8000 for her Fortune".

Lovers, like Romeo and Juliet, who tried to disobey their parents' commands, were a favourite subject in popular literature even before Shakespeare's time in the sixteenth century. But, in many cases, couples found that they fell in love after an arranged marriage. In Western society today there is usually ample opportunity for people to meet and marry whom they wish, although marriage bureaux are sometimes needed to provide the initial introduction. However, parents still choose marriage partners for their children in some countries. Even in Communist China, it was reported in 1981, 75% of marriages were "agreed upon matches". In other words, the initial introduction and financial proposals came from the parents, and the marriage proceeded if the couple liked the look of one another.

Age of Marriage

Often very young children were betrothed to each other as a result of their parents' eager-

1 An eighteenth-century marriage contract is arranged. The two fathers haggle over terms on the left, but the couple in the background look rather unhappy, in this picture by Hogarth.

ness to arrange a marriage. One fifteenth-century merchant of mature years, called Thomas Betson, advised his small fiancée Katherine to: "Be a good eater of your meat alway, that ye may wax and grow fast to be a woman." Thomas waited three years until Katherine was fifteen before they were married.

Many small children actually went through the marriage ceremony, returning afterwards to their own homes until they were old enough to live together. One extraordinary example of such a marriage took place in the Tudor period, when three-year-old John Rigmarden married a girl of five. The clergyman had difficulty in getting the right responses from John in church, and encouraged him, saying: "You must speak a little more and then go play you." An alternative to returning to their own homes was for both children to live in the boy's house, so that his mother could instruct the bride in household management. John Evelyn, the seventeenth-century diarist, married a girl aged twelve when he was twenty-seven. He travelled abroad for four years after the ceremony, leaving his wife "under the care of an excellent lady, and prudent Mother".

The accepted age for girls to marry in the sixteenth century was between twelve and fourteen. The boys were older, as they had to complete their education first. The age for girls had risen to eighteen by the nineteenth century, but can be much later today, now that women have the same education and job opportunities as men.

2 A royal marriage ceremony in the late fifteenth century. A girl might be sent to a nunnery if she had not married by the age of sixteen in the Middle Ages.

Single Women

Many girls readily agreed to an arranged marriage, as life was not easy for single women in the past. Traditionally, a girl's destiny was to marry and have children and there were few alternatives from the Middle Ages until the nineteenth century. A girl from a wealthy family in Norman England might be sent to a nunnery if she had not married by the age of sixteen. Women who lived on their own in the sixteenth and seventeenth centuries ran the risk of being thought of as witches. Girls from Tudor and Stuart middle- and upper-class families were often forced to live with relations or perhaps become a "companion" to a married relative or friend. In the eighteenth and nineteenth centuries they became governesses. The nineteenth-century novelist, Charlotte Bronte hated her "governess drudgery" and would have happily changed it for "work in the mill". It was not until the twentieth century that it began to be socially acceptable for single women to lead independent, working lives which could be as fulfilling as those of single men or married couples.

Poor Families

Although, under the feudal system of the early Middle Ages, the lord of the manor had to give his consent if one of his serf's children wanted to marry, generally, from that time until the present day, the children of the poor had much more freedom to choose a partner whom they loved. Many married to legitimize a child. Some had long engagements, particularly if one or other was away in service. Then they might meet only once a year. Flora Thompson, who writes about her life in an Oxfordshire village during the 1880s, describes these long engagements:

> ... *those who were pledged would go upstairs to write their weekly love-letter. ... They had only fourteen days happiness each year, and all the other days blank ... and this not for one year, but for six or seven or eight. Poor lovers!*

Wedding Day

In the Middle Ages the marriage service was performed at the church door, after which the couple took Mass. By the time of Elizabeth I, the ceremony took place inside the church. For poor couples, a collection, known as "bride-ale", was taken at the church, some friends bringing money and others food and drink. The wedding party was held inside the church. Wilsden Parish Church, Yorkshire, in the 1540s had two special officials appointed "to remayne in the church for to drynk in at bride-ales". This custom came to an end under the Puritans, and from 1652 a civil marriage became compulsory. Many of the old customs returned after the Restoration of Charles II, although bridal parties were now held at taverns and ale houses rather than in church.

By the sixteenth century white had become a bridal colour and a ring was used in the ceremony. Wedding cake was eaten at the party afterwards and there were many superstitions associated with it. It might be crumbled over the heads of the couple or drawn through a wedding ring as a good luck

3 An advertisement of 1897 for engagement rings. The average price for a diamond and pearl ring, like the one second from the right on the top row, was £40.

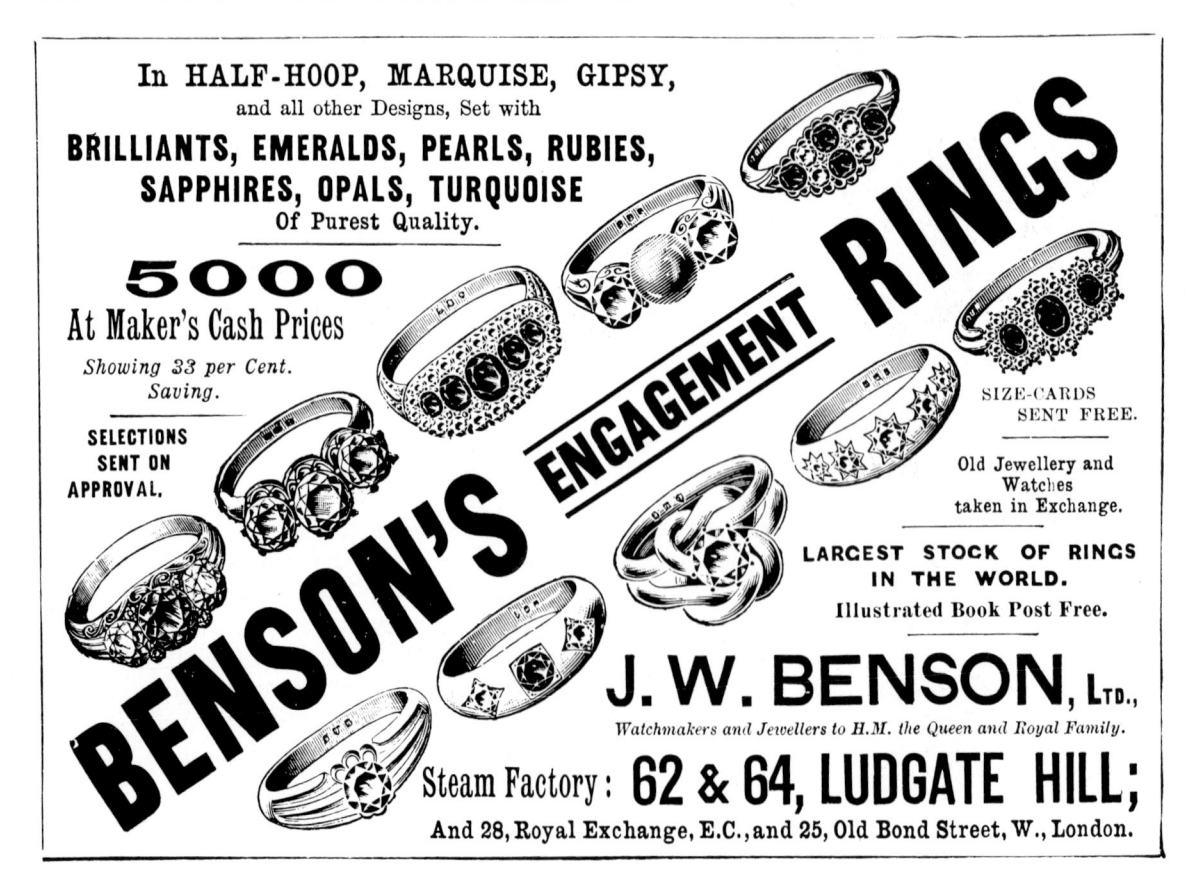

BENSON'S ENGAGEMENT RINGS

In HALF-HOOP, MARQUISE, GIPSY, and all other Designs, Set with BRILLIANTS, EMERALDS, PEARLS, RUBIES, SAPPHIRES, OPALS, TURQUOISE Of Purest Quality.

5000 At Maker's Cash Prices

Showing 33 per Cent. Saving.

SELECTIONS SENT ON APPROVAL.

SIZE-CARDS SENT FREE.

Old Jewellery and Watches taken in Exchange.

LARGEST STOCK OF RINGS IN THE WORLD.
Illustrated Book Post Free.

J. W. BENSON, Ltd.,
Watchmakers and Jewellers to H.M. the Queen and Royal Family.

Steam Factory: **62 & 64, LUDGATE HILL;**
And 28, Royal Exchange, E.C., and 25, Old Bond Street, W., London.

charm. Lady Houblon gives an account of a marriage between country gentry in September 1770 when

> *a profusion of Bride Cake was placed ready for refreshment; and salvers of rich wine, and a gold Cup containing an excellent mixture, were handed round. The Bride and Bridegroom's healths were drank, and pieces of cake were drawn properly through the Wedding Ring for the dreaming Emolument of many spinsters and Bachelors.*

5   Family life in the seventeenth century. The small child is sitting dangerously near the open fire, which is supported by curved metal firedogs in the grate.

4   A typical Victorian wedding breakfast, illustrated in the *Girl's Own Paper,* October 1897. The bride cuts the cake, and guests will enjoy sandwiches, patties, biscuits and sweetmeats, and have tea and home-made lemonade to drink.

Wedding arrangements became more elaborate in the nineteenth century, particularly among the middle classes. Girls wore fashionable wedding gowns and guests sat down to a "wedding breakfast" — so-called because all weddings took place in the morning. Poorer people just got married in their best clothes and had a less formal party. Charles Dickens describes the marriage of a painter and decorator in *Sketches by Boz*. The party was at the bridegroom's home, which was convenient, as

the bridesmaids could sit in the front parlour and receive the company, and then run into the little washhouse and see how the pudding and boiled pork were getting on in the copper.

Family Life

Women knew when they married that they could expect to have many children, most of whom would not survive until their teens. Rich families wanted heirs and the poor wanted workers to help them. As Daniel Defoe noticed approvingly in the early eighteenth century, in Colchester and Taunton:

there was not a child in the town or in the village round it of above five years old, but, if it was not neglected by its parents and untaught, could earn its bread.

Sterility was one of the worst things that could happen to a wife. Marriage was generally for life, as divorce was almost impossible before the twentieth century.

Outside amusements like the tavern, coffee house and pleasure garden were only for men or for women of doubtful reputation until the end of the nineteenth century. Respectable women did not go to restaurants on their own in the evening until the First World War. Until buses and trains started in the mid-nineteenth century, it was difficult to travel far from home. The *Girl's Own Paper* of 1901 wrote enthusiastically about the bicycle as "the greatest emancipator for women extant".

Amusements at home were limited until gas or electricity were fitted in homes. Poor families had little leisure as they worked from sunrise to sundown, and were too tired to do much afterwards. Most middle-class families had simple pleasures in the evening like reading aloud or playing the piano, until radio after the First World War and television after the Second transformed home life.

2
A House to Live In

Cottages

When a couple get married, they need somewhere to live. The cheapest houses put up in the Middle Ages were often little more than huts and have disappeared long ago. They were built from local materials which were readily available. Only the rich could afford to have stone and wood brought from another part of the country.

In Britain, up to the Industrial Revolution, most people lived in cottages, grouped together into villages. Villages grew up beside a pond or well, with a village "green". There was generally a church and manor house in the vicinity, and a windmill, where the miller ground corn for the community. People worked locally on the land and often shared their cottages with their farm animals. Industry was in the villages rather than the towns.

Many medieval cottages were built by communal effort. They were often only hovels, made from interwoven branches and plastered with a mixture of mud, straw and dung. Roofs were thatched with straw or covered with turf. Windows were very small and unglazed. There were no chimneys, and smoke escaped through gaps in the roof. Buildings of this kind were only temporary and have long-since disappeared. They cost little except in voluntary labour. They were often built on Common Land. This was allowed if the dwelling was completed in one day, with a fire burning in the hearth by sundown. Queen Elizabeth put a stop to the practice in 1589, but it continued intermittently for the next one hundred years.

Cottages which survive today from the Tudor period are those which were better built, belonging to yeomen farmers rather than labourers. They had a framework of wood, except in areas like the Cotswolds and Yorkshire, where local stone was plentiful. Most farmers rented their cottages from wealthy landowners, although some saved up sufficient money to buy them instead. Agricultural workers were relatively prosperous

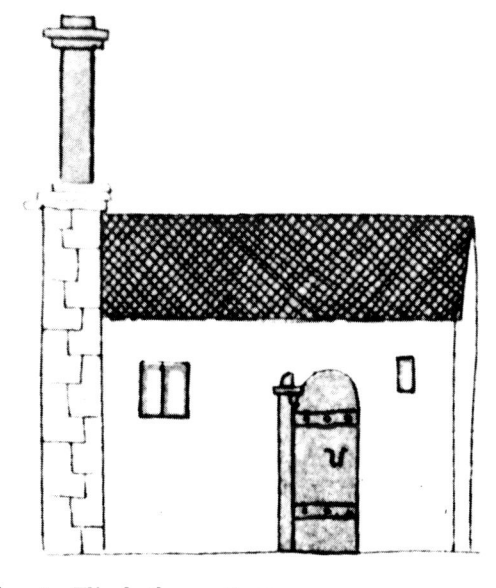

6 An Elizabethan cottage.

7 An eighteenth-century engraving of a one-storey cottage, with an outhouse for animals and a well nearby.

from the Elizabethan age until the eighteenth century, when enclosure of land and new machinery forced small farmers out of business.

Life for country people at the bottom of the social scale changed little from the Tudor period until the end of the nineteenth century. Villages were isolated, roads were bad, and transport, where it existed, was expensive. Few people travelled far from their home villages. Improvements in living conditions had to wait until running water and artificial light were connected, and, in some cases, this did not take place until well into the twentieth century. In an account of 1872, ironically named *The "Romance" of Peasant Life in the West of England*, F.G. Heath, described an agricultural labourer's cottage in the West of England. It was seven yards by three, and ten feet high.

There was, of course, no second floor to the place, and the one tiny floor was divided in the middle into two compartments, each being about three yards square.

John, the owner, was

a short, thickset man of sixty years of age.

He had lived there, he told me, a quarter of a century. His predecessors were a man, his wife and six children (a family of eight), all of whom he said had slept in the 'bedroom', nine feet square.

Cottages, like the one described, were often on one floor only. Some had an upper floor reached by a ladder.

By the 1880s, when Flora Thompson was a child, agricultural workers were less prosperous compared with the rest of the community than they had been for two hundred years. Many lived in "tied cottages" and could not change jobs without losing their homes. A Royal Commission reporting on housing in 1884 interviewed George Mitchell, who had worked on the Montacute estate, Somerset, until 1846. He said:

It is degrading to the man that is working there; he is afraid; he goes in continual fear lest he should be turned out.

Castles and Mansions

A very different life was led by wealthy families. In Norman Britain, feudal barons built fortified castles to protect themselves from robbers and rivals. Here life was communal, centring on the Hall, where family and servants ate, kept warm and slept.

As conditions in the country became more stable under the Tudors, there was less need for a fortified home. And, with new prosperity, families began to compete with each other in housebuilding. Cardinal Wolsey's palace at Hampton Court was so grand that it aroused the envy of Henry VIII himself. Numerous servants and retainers were needed to run these households. Often personal servants slept on truckle beds outside their master's bedchamber, or in one of the public rooms.

By the seventeenth and eighteenth centuries merchants, tradesmen and professional people could afford to buy large houses. Fashion played a part in the design, many of the buildings being influenced by architecture the owner had seen while on the Grand Tour. Country mansions, like the castles before them, were centres of employment for the neighbourhood. Special servants' quarters were now incorporated in the design, reached by the "back stairs".

8 Longleat House and estate, Warminster, in the seventeenth century. Now home of the Marquess of Bath, the house was first built in the mid-sixteenth century.

Town Houses

Towns in medieval Britain were still fundamentally agricultural, in spite of being centres of trade. They were encircled by a wall, and outside there was a town-field where cattle and sheep could graze. Houses were not crammed too closely together, and had their own fields round them. Buildings were constructed of wood and wattle, although there were some grander stone mansions. Streets were muddy and piled with rubbish.

William Camden's survey of England in the reign of Queen Elizabeth provides much information on the life and work of the population at that time. An average small town contained five thousand people. London had a population of two hundred thousand by 1600 and was one of the greatest trading cities in Europe. Buildings were squashed together in a random fashion, each storey protruding further into the street than the one below, in order to get more space inside. These "jettied" buildings were a fire hazard and banned by James I in the seventeenth century. There were squalid slums in Elizabethan London, known as the "rookeries", where families crowded into one room of a disused mansion, like nesting birds.

The Industrial Revolution and After

The population of England and Wales doubled in the first half of the nineteenth century and the proportion of town-dwellers rose from 20% to 54% of the population between 1801 and 1851. As a result of the Industrial Revolution, industry had moved to the towns. Existing housing could not cope with the situation, and so dreadful slums grew up in city centres. Some workers lived in rented rooms in houses specially built for the purpose, known as tenements, successors of the "rookeries". Here, in surroundings of decaying glory, families crowded together in a room measuring only 6 feet x 5 feet, which might contain nothing but a solitary bedstead.

People who lived in towns usually rented their accommodation, whether it was one room, one floor or a whole house. In Birmingham in the 1880s the average working-class wage was 27s 6d a week, and the rent cost between 15.6% and 33.3% of total income. Those with a little more money to spare rented a four-roomed house for about 11s a week, and sub-let a room for 3s. In her *Book of Household Management* in 1861, Mrs Beeton advised couples that:

> *The rent of a house ... should not exceed one-eighth of the whole income of its occupier.*

Tommy Morgan, recalling life in East End tenements at the end of the nineteenth century, said:

> *There was only one decent landlord and she was a lady. ... She kept a little shop and she let rooms out over the shop. I*

9   "Jettied" sixteenth-century houses in Chester, the top storeys overhanging the street.

used to go down there for a farthing-worth of milk or ha'p'orth of bread or anything like that, and when I went down I always paid the rent.

Although lawyers and single men had lived in "Bachelor Chambers", such as those in The Albany, London, since the seventeenth and eighteenth centuries, flats were at first not thought suitable for middle-class families. Some of the earliest privately built flats in London were Artillery Mansions in Victoria Street. They were constructed between 1852 and 1854 and consisted of reception rooms, four bedrooms and accommodation for servants. Rents were from £80 to £200 a year.

From the late eighteenth century, new houses were put up in quantity to accommodate workers crowding into the towns. The cheapest and quickest to build were "back-to-back", with one or two rooms upstairs and down. As they were joined together at the back as well as the sides, the only windows were at the front, and the interiors were very dark and stuffy. Edwin Chadwick described them in a government report of 1842:

10 "Chambers" for the legal profession in Gray's Inn, 1893.

They are built back to back; without ventilation or drainage; and, like a honeycomb, every particle of space is occupied. Double rows of these houses form courts, with, perhaps, a pump at one end and a privy at the other, common to the occupants of about twenty houses.

For skilled workers with more money, terraced houses with a small backyard or garden

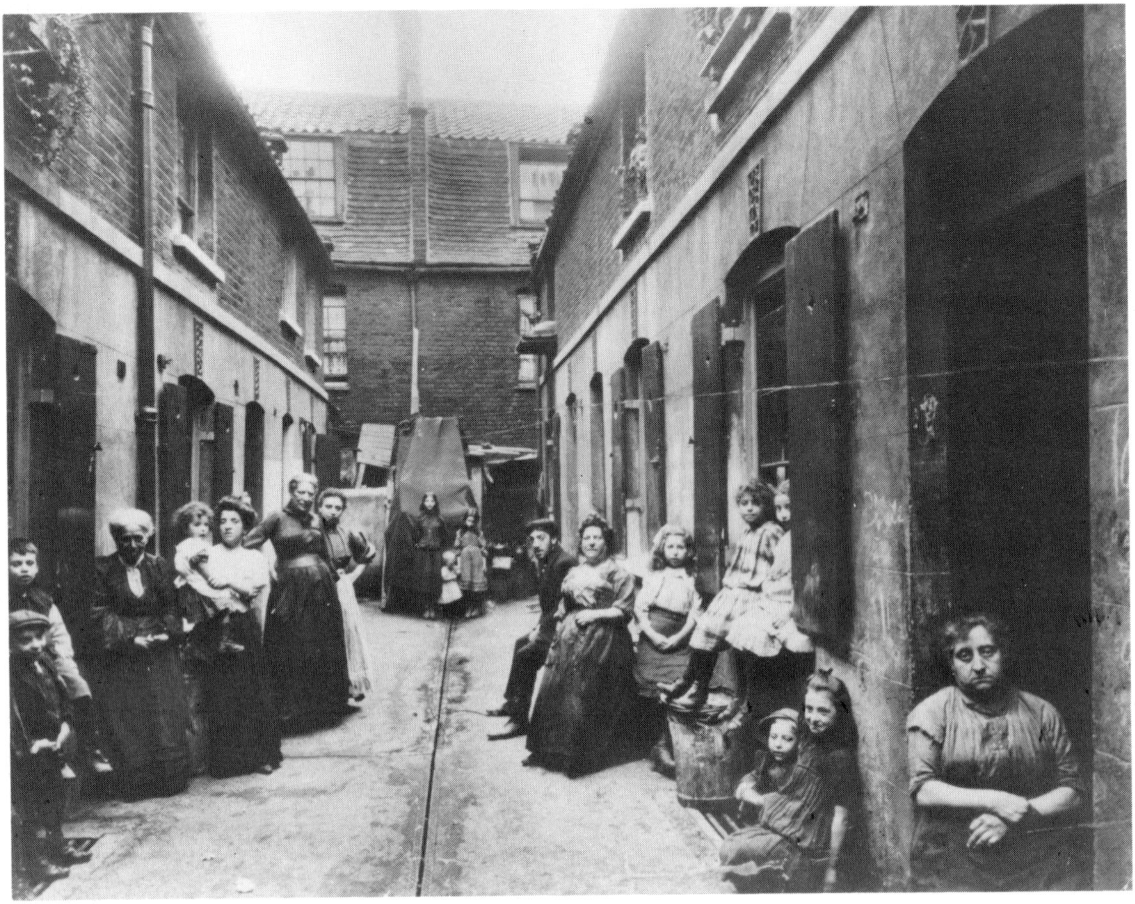

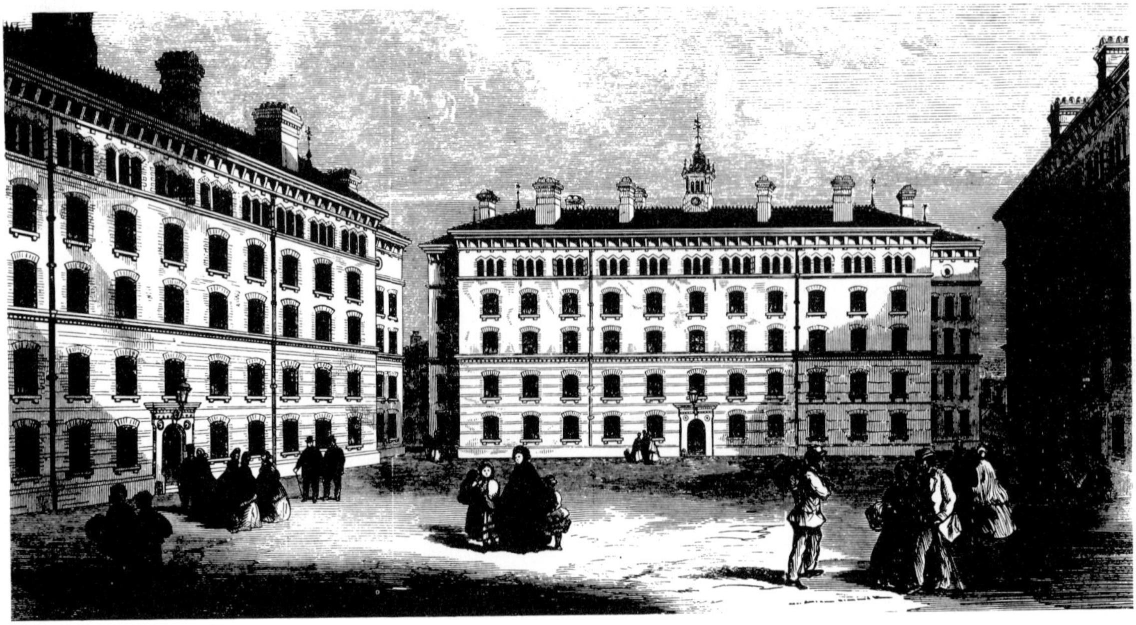

11 "Back-to-back" housing in Stepney, London, c.1909. The front doors of the terrace face onto a small alleyway. This was the most common form of workers' housing built in towns from the middle to the end of the nineteenth century.

were built. Higher up on the social scale there were dignified terraces facing onto a pleasant square, or semi-detached villas. A small number were owner-occupied. Buying a house had become easier from the 1770s, when the first "building societies" had been formed. These were originally savings clubs: members pooled their money to buy land and build houses which were allocated to members as they were ready, on the basis of a ballot. In 1800 such houses cost under £100 to build and each member of the society paid about 10s per month. A society disbanded once all its members were housed. By the 1840s building societies as we know them were being formed, offering modern-style mortgages. Members could then purchase a house immediately.

As the working classes moved into city centres in the nineteenth century, the middle classes moved out. They were able to do this because of the expansion of railway services, which enabled people to work in a town and live on the outskirts, which now became known as the "suburbs". Large towns had ever-increasing suburban areas. Mrs J.E. Panton, in her book *From Kitchen to Garret*, published in 1888, believed that the price of a season ticket to work was nothing in comparison with "being able to sleep in fresh air, to have a game of tennis in summer, or a friendly evening of music, chess or games in winter, without expense". The first suburbs were designed exclusively for the middle classes, who wanted social compatability with their neighbours. Each time the railway lines were extended, a new area was opened up for development. New "Garden Suburbs" were built, like that at Hampstead. Car ownership

12 Working-class "model" housing subsidized by George Peabody in Islington, London, 1866.

13 London Underground Railway poster advertising the pleasures of suburban life in the early twentieth century.

became more common after the First World War, as did country bus services, and so estates could be built further away from railway terminuses. Each time it was the middle class who moved out to what they considered was a more exclusive area. Only today, increases in rail fares and petrol prices are bringing people back to the cities, and "New Towns" have been built where homes and work can be near each other again.

Subsidized Housing

From the mid-nineteenth century the government tried to improve working-class housing. Minimum building standards were enforced by law from the 1870s. Some voluntary bodies, such as the Peabody Trust, put up apartment blocks in city centres for impoverished workers. Enlightened employers, like Cadbury's at Bourneville and Lever Brothers at Port Sunlight, put up "model housing" estates for their employees.

In 1918, at the end of the First World War, the government realized that private enterprise would not be able to supply sufficient houses for the returning soldiers, and grants were given to local Councils to build houses, for which the rents would be subsidized. At one new Council estate at Becontree in Essex, one of the first tenants said:

The thing that pleased us most when we first moved here was to have a house of our own, with electric light and a bathroom and a scullery with running water. We'd been in two rooms in Bethnall Green, with a tap and WC three flights down and shared with two other families. . . . I thought [the new house] was just like a palace.

3
Home Comforts

The main essentials of home life — heat, water and light — were not easily obtainable in the past. The poor had to work hard for them until the end of the nineteenth century, and the servants of the rich had to do the same.

Heating

The most important job was to look after the fire, as it was needed for warmth, cooking, and also light in the evenings. Early medieval castles and cottages had a central brazier in the main room, burning charcoal, peat or wood. As there were no chimneys, smoke had to escape through the rafters, blackening them as it went. The atmosphere was always smoky and smelt of cooking.

Once bricks were used for housebuilding in the Tudor period, it became possible to construct a fireplace and chimney. William Harrison, writing at the end of the sixteenth century, described how there were

> *old men yet dwelling in the village where I remain which have noticed . . . the multitude of chimnies lately erected.*

In 1613 the dramatist Thomas Dekker also remarked:

> *Painted chimnies in great country houses make a show afar off and catch travellers' eyes . . .*

In the mansions of the rich, fireplaces were large and jutted out into the room so that no heat would be lost. The logs were supported by firedogs, and an iron fireback protected the wall. In smaller farmhouses and cottages

14 A picture from a medieval manuscript, c. 1440, showing a man warming his feet in front of an open fire. A cooking pot is suspended over the flames and logs are neatly stacked in the background.

15 A fireside seat set into the actual fireplace of a mid-nineteenth-century fisherman's cottage. Firebricks have been put in the hearth, to convert the fire from wood to coal — which needed a draught underneath to burn.

fireplaces were often built in an arched recess, leaving seats or inglenooks for people to sit and keep warm.

The fireplace was the family gathering place in early times, so that by the Victorian period the word "hearth" had come to mean the same thing as "home". The tradition continued long after there were alternative ways of cooking and heating, and only disappeared in the twentieth century with the coming of central heating.

People were still dependent on an open fire two hundred years after the reign of Queen Elizabeth. It was generally the only heating in the house and kept alight all the year round for cooking purposes. The rich burned wood from their estates, but the poor often used peat, as they could be imprisoned for stealing wood from someone else's land. In the Victorian period, fuel cost an agricultural worker a fifth or sixth of his weekly wage.

Coal was not much used until the nineteenth century, when the railways could carry it cheaply from place to place. As coal would not burn on an open fire, fireplaces were provided with a grate off the ground, so that a draught underneath could ignite the coal. By this time many of the larger houses had fireplaces in the bedrooms, but they were inconvenient and not often used. Bedrooms were always freezing in rich and poor households alike until well into the twentieth century. Parson Woodforde recalled a particularly cold night on 28 February 1785:

The Frost severer than ever in the night as it even froze the Chamber Pots under the Beds.

16 A peaceful scene in the early nineteenth century, in front of a blazing coal fire which also heats the kitchen range on the left. Note the kitchen dresser on the right.

People had various ways of keeping warm at night. Elizabethan beds were hung with tapestries to keep out draughts. Depending on circumstances, outdoor clothes, smocks or nightgowns, and socks were worn in bed. Copper or brass warming pans were used to heat the sheets, and in the nineteenth century hot water bottles. In Flora Thompson's village in the 1880s, people brought a hot brick wrapped in a blanket upstairs. Most bedrooms were damp and people suffered from rheumatism and arthritis.

Gas heating and lighting became common in towns during the late nineteenth century, but many houses were not connected to the mains until the twentieth century. Even in towns, many of the poorer people still used open fires. Tommy Morgan, remembering his childhood in the London slums at the end of the nineteenth century, recalled:

Very rare we had a gas stove. 'Course gas was very cheap then, five hours a penny — put a penny in the slot it lasted five hours. But it was very rare we had a gas stove. Always had a coal fire. Everything on the one fireplace.

Electricity was a major benefit for families when it was finally installed as a matter of course in new houses after the First World War, although it has always been expensive compared with other fuels. Another major change came after the Second World War, when central heating was fitted in new houses

21

and flats and people were at last liberated from most of the work associated with fires. The fireplace itself disappeared as the focal point in a room, and the whole house or flat could be kept at the same temperature.

Water

Water is another essential for a householder at any period of history. In the Middle Ages every drop of water needed for drinking, cooking and washing had to be fetched by hand. Most cottages had a rainwater barrel outside, but everything else was carried from the nearest well or pond. Not everyone had a well on their own land and people might have to walk some distance. Often the water was contaminated — by dead animals or rubbish in the country, and by sewage in the towns. In summer many wells and ponds dried up, causing a serious water shortage.

Water-carrying was a woman's job and the village pump was traditionally the place for a gossip. Water was brought back home and kept in buckets in the corner of the living room. It was heated, when wanted, over the open fire. The practice continued for country people until the late nineteenth century.

Flora Thompson remembered that in her village at the end of the century only one in thirty people had piped water. The women went to the well in all weathers, "drawing up the buckets with a windlass and carting them home suspended from their shoulders by a yoke".

In the towns the situation was much the same. The poor queued up beside the nearest pump. By the end of the seventeenth century rich people could afford to pay a water company to supply their houses with water carried in wooden pipes. There were also water-carriers crying "Any fresh and fair spring water". But even in mid-nineteenth-century London the poor still had to queue up for water at a tap, which might be streets away from where they lived and was only turned on for a few minutes each day. Running water was only slowly installed in most people's houses round the turn of the century. Often it was only piped to a sink, and people had to wait much longer for lavatories and baths.

It is not surprising that bathing was something of a luxury until the arrival of piped water. In the Middle Ages bathing was communal. Water was heated in pots over the fire and family and friends got into a round wooden tub together. There were also some rather disreputable public baths in larger towns, known as "stews". By modern standards, even the wealthy did not worry too much about cleanliness in the sixteenth and seventeenth centuries. The poor washed under the pump and others managed with an ewer of water and a pewter basin in the bedroom.

Until the eighteenth century, too much washing was considered positively harmful, but then the new fashion of bathing in spa water or in the sea gradually convinced

17 Women and children collecting water from a stand-pipe in a nineteenth-century town. Stand-pipes were often the only source of water for households and might only be on for one hour a day, three days a week.

fashionable people that water was not necessarily bad for them. Fanny Burney, who kept a detailed diary of her life in the latter part of the eighteenth century, took her first plunge in the sea in 1773 and was pleased to find herself "in a glow that was delightful".

The Victorians made a positive fetish of cleanliness, believing that it was "akin to godliness". The poor were referred to as "the great unwashed". The latter had every excuse for this. Apart from the problems of carrying water, there was nowhere private to go for a wash in a small cottage. At Lancaster Cottages, a row of workmen's cottages in Richmond built in 1850, there was one well for eighteen houses. When the men came home from work, they got their wives to throw a bucket of water over them in the backyard.

Middle-class Victorian families used a tin bath, which was placed in front of the fire and filled with water by hand. Bath night was quite an event and several members of the family might use the same water. Water was heated either over the fire or else in a boiler behind it. After 1863 the installation of gas water heaters, sometimes known as "geysers", made everything much easier. All kinds of bath were designed, like the "Eureka" of 1890, which incorporated a Douche that streamed water on the bather's head, a Wave, which gushed water sideways, a Shower and a Spray. This remarkable bath could be bought for £16. By the early twentieth century mass-produced, cheap cast-iron enamelled baths became standard fittings in houses, but many families were still using the portable tin tub in the 1930s and '40s.

A mains water supply was slow to come to country cottages. In Flora Thompson's village at the end of the nineteenth century, the greatest luxury was to have a separate bath house in an out-building. A wood fire heated water in a copper container, and the water was drawn off by means of a hose pipe into the tub. Flora found it the most luxurious bath she had ever had. Looking back to her childhood, she remembered how she tried to sit,

18 These medieval women each have their own round, wooden bath tub, which would have been filled by hand. The woman in the centre, perhaps a servant, is holding a hand-mirror.

19 A Victorian bath night. The maid heats the water in a tin bath with the aid of a portable charcoal-burning immersion heater, known as "the Salamander".

with curtains drawn over the window and door and red embers glowing beneath the copper, her knees drawn up, in hot water up to her neck and luxuriate.... She was often to think of those baths in later years when she stepped into or out of the few inches of tepid water in her clean but cold modern bathroom or looked at the geyser, ticking the pennies away, and wondered if it would be too extravagant to let it run longer.

Sanitation

A constant problem for householders at all times has been the disposal of sewage. Before main drainage was gradually installed in towns from the mid-nineteenth century, there must have been a perpetual smell from sewage and rubbish. People were equally haphazard about sewage disposal in the country, but it was less offensive there, as houses and people were generally not so crowded together.

A "gard-robe" was a primitive lavatory used in medieval castles. This was only a wooden seat over a stone shaft in a draughty room. Sewage fell down the shaft into a cesspit or the moat, neither of which were often emptied. Streams and rivers were open sewers.

20 An Elizabethan herb-burner used to sweeten the air inside the house.

21 Eighteenth- to early-nineteenth-century town houses with ramshackle privies at the back, emptying into the river.

In larger houses in the sixteenth and seventeenth centuries a special room with buckets was sometimes designated as the lavatory. Some very grand commodes or "close-stools" with padded seats were used by rich families. Chamber pots were in the bedrooms. It was a servant's unpleasant job to empty these contrivances. Often the cesspit was actually in the cellar of a house, and emptied occasionally by nightsoil men. Rubbish was thrown outside in the gutter and sometimes the contents of chamber pots as well.

In the eighteenth century there was a slight improvement, as it became customary to have a privy or boghouse in the backyard or at the bottom of the garden. This was still only a wooden seat over a pit. Although a water closet had been installed in Queen Elizabeth's palace at Richmond in the sixteenth century, any effective system for ordinary people depended on the house having a piped water supply. The first modern-styled water closet was made by T.W. Twyford in 1870. For those who still had no main drainage or running water, another useful invention was the Earth Closet, designed by Rev Henry Moule in 1860. This portable closet had a reservoir containing earth. When a handle was pulled, earth was released, scouring the pan and absorbing the liquid.

In the country and in industrial slums, sanitary conditions remained very unhealthy until the end of the nineteenth century. George Mitchell, who farmed in Somerset at that time, described how many of the lavatories were far too close to the house:

> *There are holes dug in the ground, and when they are full they take the contents away into the garden. It is the only manure they have to manure their allotment with.*

Flora Thompson recalled "the hovel":

> *a little beehive-shaped building at the bottom of the garden or in a corner of the wood and toolshed.*

The closet was emptied half-yearly "which caused every door and window in the vicinity to be sealed". The contents of chamber pots were emptied on the "midden" or general rubbish dump. In the industrial slums there was generally a line of WCs at the end of the backyard, not necessarily one to each family.

Before dustmen started to call at houses weekly, there was also household rubbish to be disposed of. It was easier in the country, where all foodstuffs were put on a pile outside the house for the pig. This heap, known as the "muck'll", also smelt very bad, but it was considered to be a healthy smell. When more people came to the towns in the nineteenth century, the problems of sewage and rubbish disposal got worse. There were continuous epidemics of diarrhoea, typhus, smallpox and cholera. As a result of Edwin Chadwick's report on *The Sanitary Conditions of the Labouring Classes* in 1842, a Public Health Act of 1848 set up a General Board of Health and Local Boards to improve the public health. Among the problems tackled during the latter part of the nineteenth century were sewage and water supply. The money for improvements was provided by the rates charged to householders.

Lighting

Until the nineteenth century it was very difficult to do much close work in the evenings because of the dim light. Cottages were often quite dark in daytime as well, as they had small windows to keep them warmer. Many of the oldest forms of lighting continued to be used in some homes until the present century.

The oldest and cheapest was the rush light, first used by the Greeks and Romans. Gilbert White of Selborne, writing in 1775, said that one pound of rush-dips cost one shilling and might be made up from one thousand six hundred dry rushes. Rush lights burned for about half an hour. They were supported in a special holder made from the bark of a tree. William Cobbett, whose book *Rural Rides* recorded English life just after the Napoleonic

Wars, described in 1822 how his "grandmother, who lived to be pretty nearly ninety, never, I believe, burnt a candle in her house in her life ... she used to get meadow rushes."

Candles were more expensive than rushes, but poor people sometimes made their own. These candles did not last for long and smelt very bad. They were lit from the fire or else by means of a tinder box — a device made of wood or metal, with a metal bar on which a flint was struck. The spark from this set light to rags in the box. Safety matches, first used in the nineteenth century, made things much easier.

Another ancient method of lighting was the oil lamp. The simplest form of this was a wick burning in a container of oil. Fish oil was cheapest, but vegetable oil was used by better-off families by the eighteenth century. This was replaced by paraffin in the nineteenth century.

22 Candles cast an eerie light which may have contributed to legends of ghosts.

23 A paraffin lamp, c. 1900. Today, some of these lamps have been converted to electricity for use in modern homes.

and ceilings.

Electric bulbs were patented in 1878, by Swan in England and by Edison in the USA, but at first only the rich could afford generators. It was not until the twentieth century that generating stations were built to supply electricity to ordinary homes, and light could at last be obtained instantly by turning on a switch.

Interior Decorations

Interior decoration of houses was not much of a problem in the Middle Ages. Bare walls and earth floors were sufficient in a cottage. Rushes were spread on the floors of rich and poor homes alike, to make the rooms warmer. Sweet-smelling herbs such as bay leaves — used by Elizabeth I in her palace at Greenwich — were mixed with the rushes. This kind of carpeting was extremely unhygienic, as can be seen from a letter written by the scholar Erasmus in the sixteenth century:

The floors . . . are covered with rushes which are now and then renewed, but not so as to disturb the foundation which sometimes remains for twenty years nursing a collection of spittle, vomite, excretement of dogs and human beings, spilt beer and fish bones and other filth . . .

24 Merryweather's Catalogue for 1894 advertising new electrical appliances — curling tongs, shaving water heater, radiator and "portable fire engine".

Some parts of the room and the passages were always dark at night before the days of gas and electric lighting. The eerie light of candles and oil lamps may have contributed to legends of ghosts and bogymen. The streets outside were also dark, and people found their way about using lanterns with lighted candles inside. The first gas was used for street lighting at the beginning of the nineteenth century. In about 1842 it was piped to the first private houses, but seldom reached the villages until after its successor, electricity. Gas lighting was generally fitted only in the main rooms, either from a central fitting or from a wall bracket. From 1893 Dr Welsbach's new "incandescent gasmantle" was a popular choice for middle-class households. Gas had many disadvantages as it was noisy and smelly and sometimes stained walls

In the seventeenth and eighteenth centuries rush mats were used in cottages, and carpets began to appear on the wooden floors of mansions. The first carpets were hung on the walls out of harm's way. When they were put on the floor, they were treated with care and often covered with a "drugget" to shield them from the sun. There was also an early form of linoleum made from canvas, which had been painted and then varnished several times. Cottages generally had earth floors or flagstones until the reign of Queen Victoria, when wood began to be used.

Cottage walls only needed a coat of whitewash to brighten them. William Harrison,

25 An eighteenth-century hand-printed wallpaper.

writing in the late sixteenth century, described how the walls of mansions were "either hanged with tapestry, arras work or painted cloths ... or else they be sealed with oak". People who could not afford tapestries brightened up their walls with painted canvas or stencilled a pattern straight on to the plaster. Tudor wallpaper was designed to look as much like tapestry or embroidery as possible. It was generally put up with nails and the design printed by hand with wood blocks. During the seventeenth and eighteenth centuries flock papers became fashionable and designs with a Chinese theme. Thomas Hancock, of Boston, sending an order to London for wallpaper in 1738, wrote:

> get mine well Done and as Cheap as Possible, and if they can make it more beautiful by adding more Birds flying here and there, with some Landskips at the Bottom, Should like it well.

Wallpapers remained expensive until machine-printed papers were first produced in the nineteenth century. In any case, wallpapering was difficult in some houses as the walls were perpetually damp. A damp-proof course in houses only became compulsory in 1875.

26 An 1897 advertisement for ready-mixed paint. Earlier in the century would-be home decorators were advised to mix their own.

Couples marrying today often spend a large part of their budget on decorating their home. Household guides began to give advice on home decorating from the end of the nineteenth century, but even painting was much more difficult then than it is today as there were no proprietary brands to be bought. *Cassells Household Guide*, first published in 1869, recommends: "It is desirable, as far as possible, to mix your own paints." For the final coat

> *white-lead should be mixed to a stiff consistency with linseed oil, and rendered quite thin by the addition of spirits of turpentine. . . . The addition of a little lamp-black or Prussian-blue should not be omitted, as it greatly tends to increase the perfection of the colour.*

28

4
Furnishings

Agricultural Labourer's Cottages

Furniture used in the cottages of agricultural labourers at the lower end of the wage scale did not change much from the earliest times until the end of the nineteenth century. The living room, generally entered directly through the front door, contained the fireplace, perhaps with built-in fire seats. Little else was needed apart from a table, a chair or two, or perhaps a wooden bench. The family might own a settle, with a high back to keep off draughts. The table was used for family meals and for all household tasks. It also served as a work bench. Unless there was a separate back kitchen, all cooking pots, eating utensils, brooms and tools had to be kept in the living room. In the eighteenth and nineteenth centuries there was sometimes a built-in dresser for crockery. The staircase, if any, opened out of the living room and was small and cramped, to save space. The alcove underneath might be boarded in and used to store fuel.

The sleeping quarters generally contained a bed, but some of the family usually slept on the floor. Several people shared the bed. Some might possess a chest to store blankets and clothes, but labourers generally had few garments and so needed no special piece of furniture in which to store them.

Such furniture as rural labourers possessed might have been inherited or have been other people's cast-offs. Some people made their own furniture or employed local craftsmen. Most furniture of this kind has not survived for us to see today. Little in the way of furnishing fabrics was used. Chairs were wooden and not upholstered. Windows were small and had shutters rather than curtains. Old clothes were stuffed in the cracks to stop draughts. Cottages of this kind were typical for the lowest-paid rural workers until the twentieth century. Writing in 1872, F.G. Heath described homes at that time in the West of England:

In some cottages which I visited the rooms were almost bare of furniture. The

27 Cottage interior of the early eighteenth century. All household jobs are done in the one large living room. A rope ladder leads to the hayloft and a staircase to room upstairs for sleeping.

single bedrooms, which in many cases had to accommodate the whole family, often contained nothing but a squalid bedstead, and perhaps a small table and a broken chair, with a few ragged clothes on the bedsteads, not nearly enough to keep the poor creatures warm.

Leonard Thompson, interviewed by Ronald Blythe for his book on the history of Akenfield, recalled his life as a farmworker before 1914, when his own cottage had contained little:

There was a scrubbed brick floor and just one rug made of scraps of old clothes. . . . Six boys and girls in one bedroom and parents and baby in other. No newspaper and nothing to read except the Bible.

Furniture before the Industrial Revolution

Before furniture was mass-produced in factories, every piece was made by a craftsman. Medieval guilds, like the Guild of Carpenters and Joiners, were responsible for training apprentices. Furniture of this kind was valuable and was mentioned piece by piece in a man's will. But in the Middle Ages even a baronial castle was sparsely furnished. The essentials were chairs, table, benches, a chest for storage and perhaps beds. Early chairs could be folded up and carried from room to room. Seats for ceremonial purposes were made of stone. Single or double wooden seats, with canopies to keep out the draught, were used by the lord of the manor and his wife. These seats looked rather like choir stalls.

For dining in a medieval Hall, trestle tables were used, consisting of stout trestles and a narrow removable board. Diners sat on benches at one side of the table only, with their backs to the wall. "Joyned tables", consisting of more than one plank joined together, were being made by the Tudor period, wide enough for diners to sit at both sides.

Valuables and linen were stored in an oak chest, which could also be used as a trunk when the owner was travelling and as an extra seat at home. Early sideboards were simply chests mounted on legs and fitted with doors at the front instead of a lid on top. Small air holes were made in the sides of chests and cupboards so that they could be used for storing food left over from a meal. They became known as "livery" cupboards and were kept in the dining room or bedroom. As the evening meal was taken at five or six o'clock

28 A fifteenth-century chair, which could be folded up and taken from room to room.

29 A medieval chest where valuables were stored.

in the fifteenth and sixteenth centuries, a snack was often brought upstairs to bed at night. More elaborately carved dressers, cabinets, commodes and bureaux were made during the seventeenth and eighteenth centuries, for storage and other purposes.

At first, only the wealthy had beds. There were no special bedrooms in a Norman castle, the men generally sleeping together in the Great Hall on the tables and benches. In the Middle Ages the first bedchambers were also used as receiving rooms for visitors. The practice continued at Court during the sixteenth and seventeenth centuries; the closer advisers to the monarch were the officers of the Bedchamber. Until the eighteenth century, the lady of the house entertained her closest friends in the bedchamber or "boudoir".

The earliest beds had wooden frames with sacking stretched across the bedposts as a cover. The mattress was simply a sack filled with straw or leaves, which could be opened and remade every day if necessary. William Harrison, writing in the sixteenth century, but looking back fifty years or so, said:

Our fathers, yea and we ourselves also, have lain full oft upon straw pallets, on rough mats covered only with a sheet, under coverlets made of dagswain or hopharlots . . . and a good round log under their heads instead of a bolster or pillow.

In a Tudor household a four-poster bed, hung with tapestries, was an expensive item. The best bed was customarily left to a widow. In 1447 the Duke of Exeter bequeathed to "Anne my Wyffe . . . a bed of arras", and a yeoman, Thomas Quenell left his wife "my three beste beddes with boulsters, pyllowes and pyllowe coates belonging to them" in 1571. Bed linen was also expensive and passed down to other members of the family. By Harrison's time mattresses were filled with feathers instead of straw. Feather beds were still popular in the Victorian period, and even today feathers still make the softest pillows and warmest bedcovers.

Homes continued to be sparsely furnished in the eighteenth century. Styles in furniture changed and walnut began to supersede oak as the material used. Furniture lasted through many generations. The first upholstered chairs appeared in the reign of Charles I. These too were built to last, as many were upholstered in leather. By the eighteenth century brocade, tapestry and silk were used as furnishing fabrics. The oak settle of Tudor England was by degrees converted into a couch or settee.

The Industrial Revolution

There were great changes in home furnishing in the nineteenth century. Furniture was now made cheaply in factories. The new middle classes had plenty of money to spend and filled their homes with furniture and ornaments. The rooms of average houses were smaller than they had been and looked extremely overcrowded. Victorians liked to make their homes an outward sign of their position in life. A mid-Victorian advertisement addressed to "Those About to Marry" gives some comparative prices for furnishing houses of different sizes:

a four-roomed cottage can be completely furnished for 23 guineas; a six-roomed house completely and neatly for £70; an eight-roomed house, with many elegances and substantialities for £140; and a mansion of fourteen rooms furnished with that style, beauty and durability for which this house has obtained so large a share of public patronage, for 350 guineas.

By the end of the century there was plenty of advice in magazines on how to furnish cheaply. As *Cassells Family Magazine* counselled:

To have things tasteful and pretty costs no more than to have them ugly, but it does cost a great deal more trouble.

Some sample prices were given in the *Girl's Own Paper* in October 1897 for a couple wanting to furnish their home for £150. Among the items suggested for the drawing room were:

> *Two Chippendale elbow chairs £4. One Chesterfield sofa £10. One pillow-seated arm-chair £5. One Chippendale bureau £14. Three stained green chairs 10s 6d. One tea-table with flaps £1. One Roman carpet £2 2/-. Window seat (made by village carpenter) and upholstered £1.*

Flora Thompson noticed the changes in cottage interiors during the late nineteenth century as a result of mass production. Instead of "good, solid, hand-made furniture" there were the "cheap and ugly products of the early machine age". Pewter and brass were no longer the fashion, but in their place there were "gaudy glass vases, pottery images

30 A sparsely furnished late-eighteenth-century bedroom. A maid removes the guest's shoes. The four-poster bed has a high, feather mattress. A washstand is on the right.

31 An engaged couple buying furniture for their new home in 1903. A new sideboard like this would be an expensive item in their budget, probably costing about £12.

of animals, shell-covered boxes and plush photograph frames". Everyone had pictures on the wall. In poorer homes these were "coloured ones given by grocers as almanacs and framed at home".

In the towns the artisan classes furnished their homes according to their circumstances. They aspired to middle-class status symbols like a piano and full-drape curtains at the front window. Few couples getting married would be able to buy much new furniture, although it was considered that a "one up and one down" house could be furnished for twelve guineas at the end of the nineteenth century. Apart from chairs, table, bed, bed-linen and dressing table, also recommended as essential were a set of fire-irons (4s 6d), an ashpan (2s 11d), a washstand with tile back (£1 9s), 2 pieces of oilcloth (10s and 14s) and some rugs (about 4s each).

In the industrial slums people could afford little furniture. Robert Blatchford described the slums of Manchester in 1889, saying that the average size of rooms there was about 10 feet square. Wallpaper was "black with the grease and grime of years" and the plaster "cracked and crumbling". What furniture the inhabitants had was often left at the pawn shop for ready cash. People managed as best they could. Tommy Morgan, living in London's East End at the turn of the century, remembered that his family could never

32 Inside a working-class house, 1911. The iron grate would need frequent black-leading. A coal skuttle is beside the fire. The couple have lots of pictures and ornaments, and brightly patterned curtains and carpet.

"Listen, dear. Isn't that from 'Lohengrin'?"
"No, silly! It's from Droitwich."

34

33 A sitting room in the 1930s with one of the comparatively recent radio sets. The BBC broadcast from Droitwich in the 1930s.

afford to buy sheets. Instead his mother bought old scenery from a nearby theatre, "put it in a bath in the yard and let it soak for about a week. And when that was done two or three times we had a bedsheet."

Furniture design became more simple in the twentieth century. The cluttered look, beloved by Victorians, disappeared in the 1920s and 1930s, making housework much easier. People still bought their three-piece suite and sideboard to last a lifetime. After the Second World War, better wages and an extended use of hire purchase and credit cards enabled people to buy the furniture they wanted. Today there is little class difference in the amount of furniture in houses. The only differences are those of taste and price. There is also plenty of second-hand furniture available which is being sold not because it is worn out, but because the owners became tired of it.

34 A dining room furnished in the "Utility" style during the Second World War. Compare the sideboard on the left with the one the Victorian couple were purchasing in 1903 (picture 31).

5
Keeping House

Cleaning

A Victorian contributor to *Cassells Family Magazine* wrote in 1881:

> *dust and dirt are the worst pests of mankind, and do more to destroy health and happiness than anything else.*

This was not an overstatement if applied to homes up to the sixteenth century, when germs, bugs and lice multiplied in the filthy rushes on the floor. Traditionally, one of a housewife's jobs has always been to keep the floors clean. In medieval homes this was simply a case of sprinkling fresh rushes over the dirty ones, with a complete sweep-out every year or so. Until roads and pavements became cleaner in the eighteenth century, mud was always being brought in from outside. An Italian visiting Britain in the reign of Henry VII described how people

> *in order to remove the mud and filth from their boots, are accustomed to spread fresh rushes on the floors of all houses, on which they clean the soles of their shoes when they come in.*

Rural labourers, living in poverty in their cottages, did not worry much about household cleaning. It was the middle and upper classes who burdened themselves with housework. When wooden floors were put down in better-class houses during the seventeenth and eighteenth centuries, they needed to be scrubbed with sand and water. This was known as "wet-scouring". "Dry-rubbing" with hot sand followed, to bring up a polish on the boards. All polishes had to be concocted by the housewife as there were no proprietary brands until the nineteenth century. Even in 1877, a book on household management for brides, called *Things a Lady*

35 An Elizabethan maid doing the dusting.

Would Like to Know, gives instructions for making up polishes, such as:

> *To give a gloss to fine Oak Wainscot — if greasy, it must be washed with warm beer; then boil 2 quarts of strong beer, a bit of bee's wax as large as a walnut, and a large spoonful of sugar; wet it all over with a large brush, and when dry, rub it till bright.*

It was much easier once women could buy polishes and products like "Monkey Soap" by the end of the nineteenth century. Nowadays there are many more shortcuts, such as detergents and instant polishes. Dusting is also less of a problem than it was in an overcrowded Victorian home. It must have been almost impossible to get rid of dust in a room with a coal fire and open floorboards. Central heating and double glazing today contribute towards a dust-free atmosphere.

Carpets were not generally used as floor coverings until the eighteenth century. Before vacuum cleaners and carpet-sweepers were invented at the beginning of the twentieth century, carpets had to be taken up and beaten. Other ways of removing dust were to use a stiff carpet brush and a dustpan, or else to turn the carpet over and tread the dust out. Carpets were cleaned by sprinkling them with tea leaves and then sweeping. Carpet-sweepers were more popular than vacuum cleaners until the 1930s.

Cleaning the grate and laying the fire were daily jobs in every household until very recently. Victorian grates had to be black-leaded,

36 An Edwardian advertisement suggesting a stimulating cup of cocoa to sustain servants doing the spring cleaning.

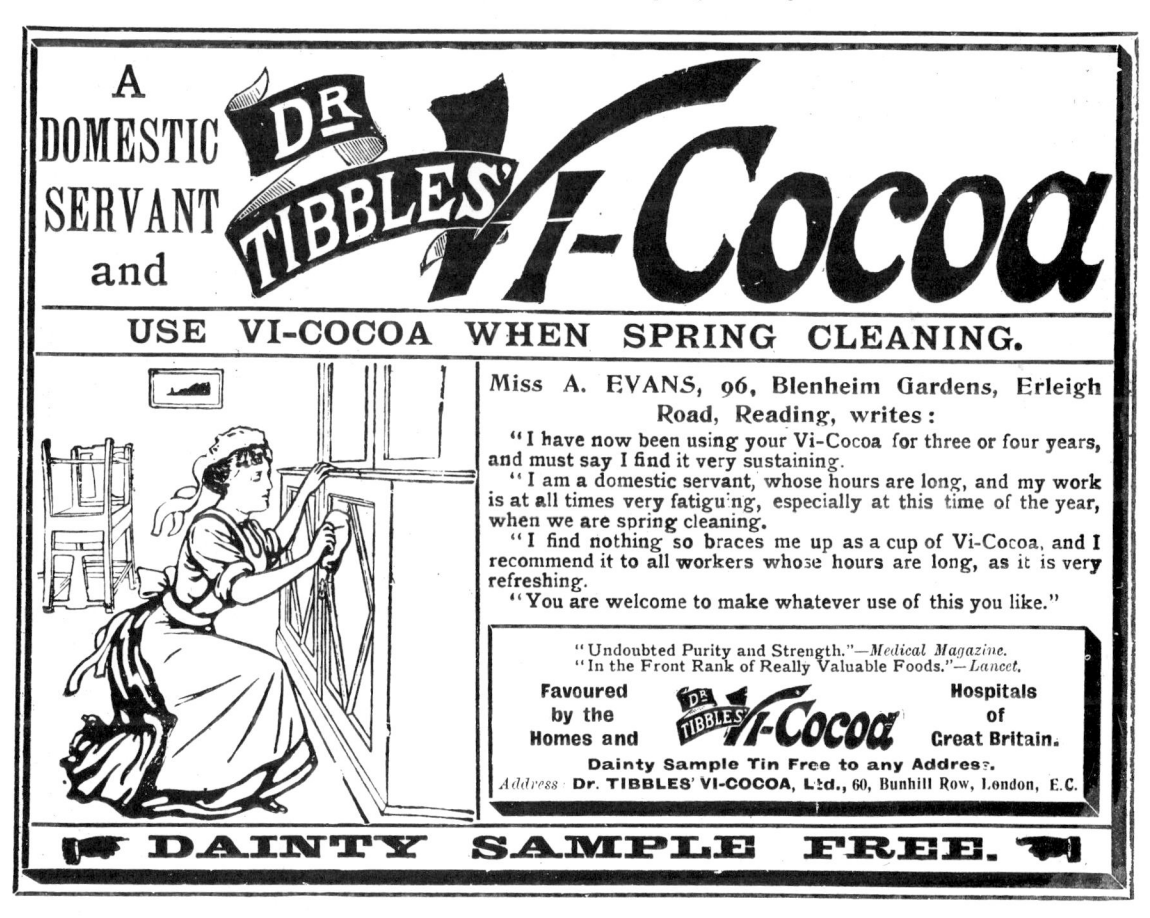

My friends know well my name is BROOKE, but yet on every hand,
In sportive familiarity, I'm called: "OLD MONKEY BRAND!"
And when they see me advertise, in various change of pose,
They smile as they remember that I WON'T WASH CLOTHES!

WON'T WASH CLOTHES.   WON'T WASH CLOTHES.

BROOKE'S
MONKEY BRAND
SOAP

FOR MAKING BICYCLES LOOK LIKE NEW.

For Polishing Metals, Marble, Paint, Cutlery, Crockery, Machinery, Baths, Stair-Rods.

FOR STEEL, IRON, BRASS AND COPPER VESSELS, FIRE-IRONS, MANTELS, &c.   REMOVES RUST, DIRT, STAINS, TARNISH, &c.

38

37 A much-advertised Victorian product for cleaning pans, polishing metals, cleaning the bath and various other household jobs. This advertisement appeared in *The Illustrated London News* in 1897.

but once tiled fireplaces became fashionable in the 1920s, things became easier.

Spring cleaning was an annual event, perhaps having its origins in the yearly cleaning-out of rushes in a medieval household. Furniture was covered in dust sheets and a very thorough cleaning job done on the floors, walls and paintwork. Paint was washed down with a mixture of soft soap, ash, sand, beer and fuller's earth, first mixed together and boiled. Wallpaper was cleaned with bread crumbs, used rather like a soft india-rubber, and windows were polished with a few drops of ammonia sprinkled on newspaper. An article in a *Girl's Own Paper* of 1923 indicates that cleaning was becoming easier, at least for the middle and upper classes:

with the improvement in electric and also hand driven appliances and their rapid incursion into homes even of the least pretentious, the entire work of spring cleaning has been revolutionised, and the biggest problem now to be solved in connection with it is how to avoid upsetting one's staff...

One practice, which helped avoid housework in the late eighteenth and nineteenth centuries, but gradually discontinued this century, was to keep a room shut up, using it only for receiving company. Furniture in this drawing room or "parlour" would be covered when not in use. Mrs Gaskell refers to this as "bagging-up" in her novel *North and South*, saying about such a room:

no one had been in it since the day when the furniture was bagged up with as much care as if the house was to be overwhelmed with lava and discovered a thousand years hence.

Laundry

A weekly wash is a recent custom. Before houses had a mains water supply, all laundry had to be washed in water carried home by hand. The alternative was to wash the clothes in a stream, beating the dirt out of them with stones or wooden bats. In the Middle Ages clothes were heavy and dyes were not fast. Wash-day in a large household might take place once or twice a year. Soap and bleach were made at home.

38 A between-the-wars advertisement for a wide variety of electrical appliances. The design of some of the fires, the toaster and the iron has not changed much over the years.

39 Elizabethan laundry maids.

By the sixteenth century some of the larger houses had a special laundry room, with a flagstone floor, where servants washed the clothes. Water was heated over a wood fire, and later in a "copper". Garments were beaten with bats, also known as "beetles". Between the sixteenth and nineteenth centuries even wealthy families only had a washing day about every three months. After washing, the clothes were dried, starched, ironed and put in lavender. Often special maids called "whitsters" came in to do the complete job.

The introduction of cotton clothes from India in the eighteenth century meant that laundering became easier. The first washing machines were invented in the nineteenth century, incorporating a corrugated washboard, known as a "dolly", such as had once been used in hand-washing to beat out the dirt. The dolly was attached to the lid of a wooden tub and turned by hand. In the twentieth century electricity was used to turn the handle in the first modern-style washing machines.

The poor washed their clothes in the kitchen sink. Those without running water sometimes used a hand-filled tub in the backyard. Smaller items of clothing were boiled in a pot over the fire. Many people did not worry much about washing their outside garments, which were made of heavy material that absorbed the dirt, and would have been difficult to wash satisfactorily, even with modern equipment.

40 A Victorian advertisement for a mangle, showing how the wet clothes were fed through rollers, turned by hand, and the surplus water drained back into the tub. Washing machines in the 1950s had rollers turned by electricity, but spin-tubs are now generally used instead to get rid of the water.

The "Ewbank-Fletcher"
With Self-Delivery Clothes Chute.

The strain of taking clothes from back of machine is done away with. Wringing or mangling is also much more quickly finished than with the ordinary Mangle.

It was hard to wring the water from washing by hand. Although an early clothes wringer had been invented by Sir John Hoskins in the seventeenth century, the first effective wringers, known as "box mangles", were not generally used until the early nineteenth century. They were very heavy and consisted of a heavy wooden box which travelled backwards and forwards over rollers, with the clothes wound through them. In the nineteenth century "mangles" became lighter and the clothes were fed into rollers operated by a wheel. Mangles have never been a very good way of removing water from clothes, as they are inclined to tear them and break off buttons.

The first irons were hollow, and known as "flat irons". They were heated by placing them over the fire. Clothes were ironed on the living room table covered with a blanket. Depending on fashion, there were many ironing and finishing devices from the Tudor period onwards. Mid-sixteenth-century ruffs required starching and then crimping, or pressing into small pleats, with a "poking stick". This device was later known as a "goffering iron" and consisted of a hollow metal stick on a stand, heated by putting a hot metal rod inside. A linen press was used to put creases into heavy fabrics. In the twentieth century everything of this kind came to be powered by electricity.

Wash-day was always a big event. Tommy Morgan remembered the early years of the twentieth century in the East End:

Always done it at home in a bath on two chairs, same bath as we bathed in she used to wash the clothes in.

Flora Thompson remembered her employer, Miss Lane's

middle-class country custom of one huge washing of linen every six weeks. In her girlhood it would have been thought poor looking to have had a weekly or fortnightly washday.

In other words, a six-weekly wash showed that she had plenty of changes of underwear. Miss Lane had a small detached building, known as the "wash house", and hired a washerwoman for two days to do the job. The washerwoman arrived at 6.00 am on Monday morning and left on Tuesday evening with 3s in wages. During the rest of the week the family folded, sprinkled, mangled, ironed and aired the clothes. Garments were aired in front of the fire on a "clothes horse" or placed on an overhead wooden airer. Electric tumble dryers and heaters made things easier from the 1950s on.

Food and its Preparation

Marketing and preparing food have been major responsibilities for housewives through

41 A drawing by Edward Ardizzone showing people in a laundrette, c. 1962. Laundrettes, which are generally open day and night, have become quite a social centre for people who have not got their own washing machine.

the ages. Country wives also had to work in the dairy, brew ales and look after domestic animals. The domestic economy of rural labourers from the earliest times depended on the family pig. Often the family only ate meat when the pig was slaughtered. Flora Thompson describes how the "family pig was everybody's pride and everybody's business". Often an arrangement was made with the baker or miller that

he should give credit now, and when the pig was killed receive a portion of meat in payment. More often than not one-half the pig meat would be mortgaged in this

42 Rural domestic economy depended on the family pig. In this illustration from a seventeenth-century calendar, a couple are slaughtering the pig, and in the background the next stages of butchering and curing can be seen.

way and it was no uncommon thing to hear a woman say, 'Us be going to kill half a pig, please God, come Friday', leaving the uninitiated to conclude that the other half would still run about in the sty.

It was difficult to keep a pig in town, but almost everyone kept chickens. This habit got a new lease of life during the Second World War, when it was the only way you could get fresh eggs.

The storage of food has been a constant problem over the centuries. Farm animals were slaughtered every winter in the Middle Ages, and the meat had to be preserved. Once it was discovered in the seventeenth century that turnips would provide winter feeding for the animals, the animal slaughter did not take place, but food still had to be kept fresh for some period of time. Hams were smoked over the open fire and then hung from the ceiling in farmhouses and cottages. Other meat was kept in barrels filled with salt. Fruit for preserving was placed in earthenware jars and covered with boiling water. From the eighteenth century, when sugar was imported from the colonies, fruit was sometimes crystallized instead. Herbs were dried and hung up. Meat was often bad, in fact, when it was eaten; in wealthier households the taste could be disguised by using spices. Parson Woodforde mentions a disastrous dinner party on 17 June 1777, when his guests were forced to eat "a bad Leg of Mutton boiled scarce fit to be eat by being kept too long". The only way to keep fresh food was to use a "larder" — included in country mansions from the seventeenth century and in most larger houses by the Victorian period. A larder was a food cupboard, generally big enough to walk inside, placed on the cooler side of a house. There was a stone floor to keep it cool, and air-holes in the wall to the outside. Richer families in the same period sometimes had an "ice house" in the garden, underground, where it was cooler. Victorian families were able to buy ice to make icecreams at home, but it would not last very long unless put in the ice house.

Before tea and coffee began to be imported widely in the eighteenth century, women of the household had to brew beers and ales at home. Children at the time of Queen Elizabeth drank "small beer", from a second brewing after the stronger beer had been drawn off. Ales and country wines were made from local herbs, fruit and vegetables. The Elizabethans even had a brew known as "cock", which was ale in which a cockerel had been steeped.

Cooking

Originally, all cooking was done in a pot or on a spit over the open fire. Peasant families often had no spit but would grill small pieces of meat on a "gridiron" by the fire. Frying pans used on open fires had long handles. Medieval ovens were simply a hole in the back of the fireplace with an iron door. A wood fire was burnt inside and the ashes then raked out. Bread or a cooking pot could then be put in and it was hot enough for the food to cook. Poorer people used a metal box, later known as a "dutch oven", which could be put directly on the fire or in the ashes.

43 A sixteenth-century stewpot or casserole, with feet to stand in the embers of an open fire.

Bread would sometimes be baked on the stones surrounding the fireplace.

In 1780 a new invention by Thomas Robinson caused a revolution in cooking habits. Robinson invented a kitchen range, and by the early nineteenth century most people had adopted this system of an enclosed fire, plus oven. Often water was also heated from the fire in a boiler at the back of the range. New cooking utensils were needed for kitchen ranges. Instead of the old "skillet", a long-handled metal pot with three legs which was used on an open fire, the new saucepans and frying pans had shorter handles and flat bottoms, without legs. At the end of the nineteenth century a new material called "aluminium" started to be used for pots and pans. It was light and much easier to clean than iron or copper. In recent years the greatest change in cooking utensils has been the use of a "non-stick" surface.

When gas was first connected to the main towns, it was used only for lighting. The first gas-powered cookers were introduced in the 1830s and '40s. They were made of cast iron, and, later, white enamelled sides and doors were added to them. Gas remained expensive for cooking until the 1920s. Electricity cost still more, and was not widely used until after the Second World War.

Alternative cooking arrangements for poor families were the paraffin stove or "Primus".

44 Edwardian schoolgirls learning to cook on a kitchen range. A box of salt is on the wall on the right of the cooker.

44

Another old method was the "hay-box". For this, a fire-proof covered pot, known as a casserole, was filled with food heated to boiling point. The casserole was then put into a box and surrounded with hay to keep the food simmering. Even in 1911 the *Girl's Own Paper* was suggesting the use of a "fireless cooking-box", using hay, for economical cooking. Its successor today is the electric "Slow Cooker", which works on the same principle.

The variety of household gadgets which are available today have greatly increased the speed with which food can be prepared. Many hand-driven appliances were introduced in the Victorian period, such as an egg whisk, a mincing machine and a coffee grinder. Just before the First World War, *Everywoman's Encyclopedia* ran a feature on electrical gadgets for those lucky enough to have mains electricity. Some inventions like coffee percolators, hot-plates, kettles and chafing dishes were recommended for flat dwellers. At that time an electric kettle could be bought for half a guinea.

Eating Utensils

Utensils used at meals varied little in shape over the centuries. Up to the fifteenth century, in poorer households, meat was served onto squares of bread known as "trenchers". These were later replaced with wooden platters and bowls, which were cheap to make and almost indestructible. From the seventeenth century, pewter, tin and then pottery and china replaced wood, although wooden trenchers survived in the country until the twentieth century.

Glass was too expensive for drinking vessels until the eighteenth century. Horn drinking tumblers and pewter tankards were used in the sixteenth century and earthenware mugs were a cheap substitute later. A Frenchman who visited England in 1558 wrote:

they do not drink . . . out of glasses, but from earthen pots with silver handles and covers, and this even in houses of persons of middling fortune; for as to the poor, the covers of their pots are only pewter . . .

Cutlery at first consisted only of a knife and spoon, made of metal. The most expensive was made of silver, or silver covered with a thin layer of gold. People carried their utensils about with them, as they were valuable. Until the seventeenth century it was the custom for people to help themselves at table, using the point of their knives, and dipping their spoons into the communal bowl of broth. Forks were first introduced from Italy, at the end of the seventeenth century, and originally had only two prongs.

The only changes in eating utensils during the last two hundred years have been in materials. Pewter and tin were discontinued in favour of china and pottery, which was widely produced in factories after the Industrial Revolution. In the nineteenth century the invention of stainless steel for cutlery made cleaning easier, and plastic is now used for some crockery, which is at least cheap and unbreakable, although not very beautiful or lasting.

45 Pewter plate and drinking tankards, from Tudor times.

46 This Elizabethan family eat with spoons from wooden trenchers. Bread rolls are put straight onto the wooden table. Father and mother sit at either end of the table and the younger children stand up to eat.

Meals

In Norman Britain dinner was at mid-day and was the main meal of the day. Breakfast was scanty and supper was at sundown. Gradually, the evening meal became the most important one of the day. Agricultural workers ate very little until then, having a snack in the fields at lunch time. An agricultural worker called George Mitchell recalled that in the 1830s he

> sometimes would pull a turnip in the fields and gnaw it to prevent hunger gnawing me. If I could find peas, beans or acorns, I would eat as many as I could get, and many a time have I hunted and foraged about for snails in the hedges and roasted them for my lunch or tea.

The evening meal in Flora Thompson's village in the 1880s was known as "Tea". It was the only hot meal of the day, and vegetables, a roly poly and a small piece of bacon were all cooked together in one pot. A roly poly was an essential item of food for poor families in the nineteenth century. It was made of flour and suet formed into a dough with water, and rolled up like a Swiss roll with a sweet or savoury filling. Then it was tied up in a cloth and boiled. It was cheap, and a good way of making small pieces of meat or vegetables go further.

The poor in the nineteenth-century industrial slums did not necessarily fare too badly. Butchers sold off meat cheaply at the weekend in case it went bad. A free meal could sometimes be obtained at the mission hall or a soup kitchen, run by the Salvation Army or other charitable institutions for the poor.

The rich in the past ate much larger meals than we do today. Samuel Pepys has left many accounts in his diaries of dinner parties held by his family at the beginning of the seventeenth century. On one occasion they gave their friends oysters, followed by "a hash of rabbits and lamb, and a rare chine of beef". This was followed by "Roasted fowle", finishing with tart, fruit and cheese, the whole meal costing about £5 for eight people. Parson Woodforde was very fond of his food, and left detailed accounts of dinner parties. On 13 September 1766 he and three guests dined off "a dish of Tench, Ham and Fowls, roasted Leg of Mutton and an Apples Pudding", with "Wine, Punch, Beer and Cyder to drink". Victorian and Edwardian diaries are full of accounts of elaborate breakfasts, as well as other heavy meals, including tea. Breakfast in the country home of a wealthy family was often an enormous meal, as it was eaten after everyone had been at work for several hours. It might consist of devilled kidneys, ham, game pie, steaks, eggs and bread. The Victorian book on household management, called *Things a Lady Would Like to Know*, encourages its readers to be more moderate: typical December breakfast menu suggestions are Dried Sprats Rump Steak Pie and Potted Shrimps, and tea, coffee or cocoa, "good bread and sweet butter, together with a fitting supply of milk and cream."

The greatest change in eating habits in the twentieth century has been the introduction of convenience foods. Tinned food, frozen food and even products like custard powder have all made cooking simpler. An eighty-five-year-old called Fred Mitchell expressed his views about this when he was interviewed by the author of *Akenfield* in 1969:

> *My wife made her own bread and there was something cooked every day, no matter how broke we were. She was a great hand at long puddings with plenty of suet and lemon peel in them, which she made in a boiler. Today, they make a dinner out of nothing. You can hear the paper packs being torn open and in five minutes it's dinner. I don't call that dinner.*

Servants

The most obvious difference between a middle-class household in the 1850s and one in the 1980s is the lack of servants today. There are now all kinds of mechanical gadgets and shortcuts to housekeeping. In the past, labour was cheap and domestic service was considered a good job, particularly for a woman. As late as 1901 the *Girl's Own Paper* was recommending girls to go into service, as a cook could get between £25 and £50 a year plus "tea, fire, no small item these days, lodging and washing without cost to herself".

Homes of the wealthy needed armies of servants to keep them going. In the Middle Ages the distinction between the higher servants and their masters was not so defined as it later became. Many of the servants in higher appointments became a lord's trusted friend. Families sent their sons to the households of friends, to be trained to wait at a lord's table. Poor relations were taken on, and the children of local merchants. Some servants were left legacies by their employers, and others did even better. Bess of Hardwick served in the households of the Zouches and the Greys before a series of marriages, among them to Sir William Cavendish and to George Talbot, 6th Earl of Shrewsbury, made her a Countess and later founder of two dukedoms, in the sixteenth century. The Duchess of Suffolk married her "gentleman usher" in 1553 and a few years later her stepdaughter

47 An eighteenth-century footman brings in the roast beef.

married her master of horse. Even in smaller households during the seventeenth and eighteenth centuries, retainers were chosen from respected families in the neighbourhood.

From the servant's point of view, it was better to be employed in a large household than a small one. There was more status and money was better. The worst was to be the sole servant in a small household — maid-of-all-work. There was a rigid hierarchy in the servants' hall. A nineteenth-century American visitor, Elizabeth Bancroft, remarked on this:

A lady's maid is a very great character indeed, and would be much more unwilling to take her tea with, or speak familiarly to, a footman or a housemaid than I should. My greatest mistakes in England have been committed towards those high dignitaries my own maid and the butler, whose grandeur I entirely misappreciated.

An early book of advice on how to deal with servants was written in 1675 by Mrs Hannah Wolley. She advised the wife to keep a close check on accounts and to oversee all work, and always to warn a servant first, if behaviour was unsatisfactory. On dismissal, do not give her "too ill a character" (reference) as it will "raise you little benefit, although it may lay the basis of her utter ruin". A special book of advice to servants, called *The Servant's Behaviour Book*, was published in the nineteenth century, and included the recommendations:

Never let your voice be heard by the ladies and gentlemen of the house except when necessary, and then as little as possible. . . . Do not ever choose gay patterns or colours. Not only are such dresses unfit for morning work, after they are a little worn, but they can never look becoming for servants . . .

Servants worked a very long day. Their wages were small, but could be saved as they had no living expenses. In 1685 a Sussex squire employed Abraham Holford as a footman for 30s a year, with clothes and board provided. At the same time the chambermaid and cook received 50s a year each and the coachman had £6, plus 2s 6d more "for catching moles", an unusual extra job for the driver of a coach and horses. Servants employed in London were generally paid more than in the country. In the eighteenth century servants working in fashionable London homes often wore cast-off clothes given to them by their masters and copied their way of life. Menservants accompanied their employers to the theatre and other places of amusement and had a social life of their own.

The middle classes could afford to employ servants in the nineteenth century. Mrs Beeton advised anyone with an income of £1,000 a year to have a cook, upper housemaid, nursemaid, under housemaid and a

48 A gadget for boot-cleaning — a job performed by the "Occasional Boy" in large Victorian households.

49 A Victorian nursemaid, employed by even the most modest households to look after the children.

manservant. Even a family earning £150 a year could afford a maid-of-all-work. A girl working as a live-in general servant in 1901 would expect £6 a year if she was under fifteen, £17 between age sixteen and twenty and £20 by age thirty-five. Out of this, she would expect to have four or five pounds "of her very own", as the *Girl's Own Paper* put it, "to buy necessary clothing, put away in the savings bank or help her people at home".

Before the First World War many servants had enjoyed the protection gained by working for a family. Often, married couples worked together, their children automatically becoming servants in the same household when they got older. But both men and women were less inclined to go into service after the war, as they disliked the loss of freedom. Ex-gardener Christopher Falconer, interviewed by Ronald Blythe for *Akenfield*, found conditions irksome, when he returned to his cottage on a big estate after the war. The cottage was without running water, a bath or electricity, and when his employers insisted that his new wife should work at the big house as a maid, he decided that it was time to find another job.

Even before 1914 some people were employing daily maids or "charwomen" for rough work. This became more common for middle-class households between the wars, although the upper classes still managed to maintain households of live-in servants. Today, people are more inclined to get occasional help from an agency or manage by themselves.

6
The Consumer Society

Attitudes to homemaking completely changed in the nineteenth century. The consumer goods produced as a result of the Industrial Revolution found a market in the new middle classes, who had money to spend and wanted advice on how to spend it. The range of goods available to a nineteenth-century shopper would have been impossible for someone born in the early eighteenth century to imagine.

Travelling Salesmen

In the Middle Ages there were few permanent shops. Country people did not travel far and relied on nearby markets or fairs, or the travelling pedlars for food and luxuries.

"Callers" were still coming round with goods in Flora Thompson's childhood. Some came regularly with essentials like potatoes, fruit and fish. The baker also called three times a week, and many other casuals passed through the village. There were tinkers calling "Any razors or scissors to grind" or "Any old pots or kettles to mend". Gypsies came to the door with clothes-pegs and told fortunes. Tramps were a familiar sight on the road until the Second World War. Some had goods to sell, but mostly they begged for food and clothing. These travelling salesmen in the 1880s must have been similar to the pedlars and packmen who roamed the villages with their goods in the Middle Ages. In the sixteenth and seventeenth centuries pedlars sometimes stayed the night at a house, and, this way, people could hear news of the outside world. A travelling tailor might call, and stay on until his work was finished. Parson Woodforde mentions a visit from a Mr Aldridge on 16 April 1782, "who carried about cottons, Linens, Muslins, Lace, Holland, etc in a Cart and comes round regularly once in ten weeks".

50 Pedlar dolls from the beginning of the nineteenth century. The woman sells kitchen utensils, including graters and toasting forks, and a lantern, a candlestick and lots of string bags and rope. The man carries luxury items: for example, beads, ribbons and scent.

Shops

Shops in the towns were generally only temporary constructions until the Elizabethan period. The first permanent shops were goldsmiths and silversmiths selling luxury goods and the bakers and farriers who supplied essentials. They were situated in the market place of a town. Traders lived above the premises with their apprentices. Little could be displayed, as shop fronts were not glassed over. They were open-fronted and closed with shutters at night. Transport was difficult and few country people even visited their local town.

By the eighteenth century, people could get about more easily by using the regular mail coach services between towns. Carts carrying farm produce, known as "country carriers", also kept to a timetable, and brought people in to town from the villages. Shops dealing in luxury goods opened in the bigger towns, but were generally patronised only by the rich and fashionable. A visitor to London from Germany, in 1768, called Sophie von la Roche, was enchanted by the Oxford Road shops:

> *First one passes a watchmaker's, then a silk or fan store, now a silversmith's, a china or glass shop. . . . Just as alluring are the confectioners and fruiterers, where, behind the handsome glass windows, pyramids of pineapples, figs, grapes, oranges and all manner of fruits are on show . . .*

Many more shops opened in the nineteenth century, and transport improved so much that a correspondent to the *Lady's World* could write:

> *Now that the train service is so perfect between London and Bath, it is quite possible to spend a day in town and return to Bath the same evening.*

In 1909 Selfridges, one of the new department stores, opened, inviting families to spend a day out in the shop.

Not everyone had enough money to buy the goods they wanted. The "tallyman" or "Johnny Fortnightly" is a well-known figure in Dickens' novels. Flora Thompson remembers such a man in her home village in the 1880s. He owned a furniture shop in a town nearby and tried to sell things on the "instalment plan". The attraction was that goods could be obtained by a small down payment, followed by weekly instalments. Many villagers ordered zinc baths and washstands from him, which they did not really need, for 1/6 a fortnight. The salesman continued calling "until he had collected as much as he thought possible and then disappeared from the scene", as most people found it impossible to keep up with the payments. The tallyman was the forerunner of hire purchase, credit cards and other methods of delayed payment.

In the twentieth century shopping has been made even easier for people. Before the

51 The grocer's "boy", off to deliver cakes, on his tricycle in the early 1930s.

52　Sculptures of two elegant women shoppers in a modern shopping area, Knightsbridge, London.

Second World War goods could be ordered from a shop by telephone and delivered to the house. Since the war delivery of grocery orders has almost ceased. Larger items of furniture are still delivered, and shopping by mail order catalogue has become popular. A much wider variety of goods are available for customers which they can see on display in supermarkets, in advertisements, and on television.

Advertising

In the nineteenth century manufacturers had to compete for the customer's attention, particularly as many of the goods they were selling were luxuries rather than essentials. The great age of poster design was the nineteenth century. Through the development of colour lithography in the 1860s, impressive pictorial posters could now be produced. Even more important became the advertisements in newspapers and pictorial journals. The first regular illustrated paper, *The Illustrated London News*, commenced publication in 1842, and was followed by numerous magazines, all of which carried advertisements. There was no code of practice for advertisers and many made exaggerated claims for their products. New magazines like *Cassells Household Guide* were published for homemakers, and publications such as the *Girl's Own Paper* had regular features about household problems.

The power of advertising grew stronger in the twentieth century, with radio, film and television, and it can often be said to persuade people to buy something that they do not really want.

◀ 53 The title page of an Edwardian women's magazine. Articles on the home and marriage combined well with advertisements for household products.

54 A late-nineteenth-century advertisement for Bovril. Although the figure of the Pope was used to recommend the product, it is doubtful whether his permission was ever obtained.

7
A Classless Society

Domestic life, as well as a great many other things, was transformed as a result of two world wars in the twentieth century. The gap between social classes in housing, clothes, food and general standard of living was gradually narrowed, and the employment of married and single women in war work meant that the pattern of life inside the home also altered.

Food

The German submarine blockade in the First World War soon created shortages of all kinds in Britain. Prices of essential foods like bread, potatoes and tea, which had once been cheap, rose sharply. By 1917 a loaf of bread was twice the pre-war price. Long queues formed when food in short supply arrived in the shops. *The Observer* described in April 1917 how a wagon loaded with potatoes was "surrounded by hundreds of clamouring people, chiefly women who scrambled to the vehicle in eagerness to buy. Several women fainted in the struggle, and the police were sent to restore order." To ensure a fairer method of food distribution, the government introduced rationing for sugar and fats in 1917, followed by more items in 1918. As a result of rationing, some families actually had more to eat than they had had before the war.

War-time legislation restricting the sale of drink had an unexpected effect on working-class budgets, making more money available to buy food. Before the war one of the few

55 Second World War government poster by Fougasse.

pleasures available to the working man had been drink. In February 1915 the Minister of Munitions, Lloyd George, declared: "Drink is doing us more damage in the war than all the German submarines put together." The Licensing Acts of 1915, 1916 and 1921 restricted the hours when alcohol could be sold, and in 1918 one Scottish Chief Constable reported:

Non-licensed grocers and other shopkeepers say that they have never done so good business amongst the working classes on Saturdays. This they believe to be due to the fact that working men get home with their wages, which they hand over to their wives, and partake of a proper meal prior to the opening of licensed premises.

Men as well as women could not find jobs during the economic depression which followed the war and there was little money available for feeding the family. When war broke out again in 1939, a comprehensive rationing scheme was put into force by Lord Woolton, Minister of Food, who guaranteed that everyone would receive "the minimum amount of proteins and vitamins necessary to ensure good health under hard working conditions". Housewives were told to register with a specific grocer, butcher and dairy to buy their rations, obtainable only by showing their ration books. Amounts of food allowed varied during the war according to availability. In July 1940, for instance, one person's allocation of butter and cooking fats per week was 2oz. In July 1941 the cheese ration for the same period was only 1oz. Meat was very scarce and a single person's allowance small, which meant that only large families could collect enough coupons together for a Sunday joint. Offal and fish were off the ration, but hard to find. The government issued Food Education leaflets suggesting recipes for meatless dishes like "Woolton Pie", consisting of vegetables in brown gravy, under a pie crust.

It was difficult to make a cake when there was no dried fruit, glacé cherries or icing sugar for sale. Wartime recipes suggested substituting lard for butter, custard powder or dried egg for fresh eggs, and golden syrup for sugar. Cream disappeared for the duration of the war, giving way to "mock cream", consisting largely of cornflour. Newspapers and magazines gave endless advice on the making of such delicacies as Carrot Jam, Bread Soup or Wartime Trifle (a stale teabun, fruit juice and custard, made with potato flour, plus flavouring).

Conditions were slightly better in rural areas. London children evacuated to the country sometimes fared better than before the war. "Here we have Sunday dinner every day," one said. Some kinds of food remained on the ration until 1954, helping to raise the nutritional standards of all classes and doing away with some of the pre-war inequalities. During the post-war period the government also organized free distribution of supplements to diet, like orange juice and milk, which were considered essential for all pregnant women and children of school age.

Housing and Living Conditions

Bad housing, like malnutrition, had been a great social evil before the First World War. In 1913 the Prime Minister, Asquith, estimated that the shortage of houses in Britain was between 100,000 and 120,000. Slum conditions were very bad, particularly in the North and in Scotland. During the war housebuilding virtually came to a standstill, but it became first priority after the Armistice. The government pledged itself to provide "Homes Fit for Heroes". Through the 1919 Housing and Town Planning Act, local councils were made responsible for deciding on housing needs in their areas. The government would then provide most of the finances for building. Rents charged to council tenants were subsidized. Regulations ensured that the new homes all had bathrooms and good-sized living rooms. The most popular type of house built after the war, by council as well as private builders, was "semi-detached". Some small blocks of flats were also put up.

Between the wars the outskirts of towns and main roads were lined with new housing estates. Semi-detached houses, each with a small garden, although pleasant to live in, took up a lot of space and people had to live further and further away from the town and their place of work. The new suburbs, therefore, each had their own row of local shops. There was little difference in living conditions between people in cheaper, privately owned houses and their neighbours on council estates.

After the Second World War there was another serious housing shortage, because of the destruction of so many buildings by bombing. Housebuilding was again first priority under Attlee's Labour government in 1945. Architects believed that tower blocks of council flats were the most suitable form of building on bomb sites in city centres and on the outskirts of towns. Tenants missed the old intimacy of small streets, where they had gossiped with neighbours over the garden wall, but, with central heating and consistent hot water, the new flats were more luxurious inside than most pre-war private or council housing. Flats were also popular for private purchasers in the fifties and early sixties, but these blocks were generally smaller.

The Welfare State

Unemployment between the two world wars, brought about by a world trade recession, caused hardship and distress, particularly in the North of England. By 1933 almost three million were unemployed and conditions did not improve until war broke out again in 1939. As a result of the National Insurance Acts of 1911 and 1920, some health insurance money was payable if a man was off sick from work, and there was government assistance for the unemployed, but the amounts paid were pitifully low. Unemployment relief was known as the "dole" and could be obtained by signing on regularly at the Labour Exchange. In 1930 a married couple with two children received only 30s a week. *Picture Post* published the budget of a typical unemployed skilled worker on 21 January 1939. Alfred Smith lived in the basement of a tenement in Peckham, which cost him 14s 6d a week, about 30% of his income. He paid 6s into a Clothing Club, 1s 8d on Insurance, 2s for a Coal Club, 1s for Coke, lighting cost him 3s and food £1 2s. His Unemployment Benefit amounted to £2 7s 6d, leaving a deficit of about 4s a week. Wives keeping house on the "dole" somehow had to provide cheap, filling meals for their families. Big items like fuel or clothing could only be paid for by putting a few pence into a Club savings scheme each week, and drawing out the money perhaps once a year.

A lasting improvement in living conditions after the Second World War was due to the development of the Welfare State. The Beveridge Report, published in 1942, outlined proposals for a new Britain, with adequate housing, and food and medical care for everyone. The National Health Act of 1948 was the cornerstone of the new Welfare State, providing for free medical care, family allowances, unemployment benefit and old age pensions. As a result, the fear of poverty and starvation was removed, and living conditions improved for the poorer members of the population.

56   Post-war block of council flats, behind a group of prefabricated houses put up as temporary accommodation during the Second World War, but remaining in use for a good many years afterwards.

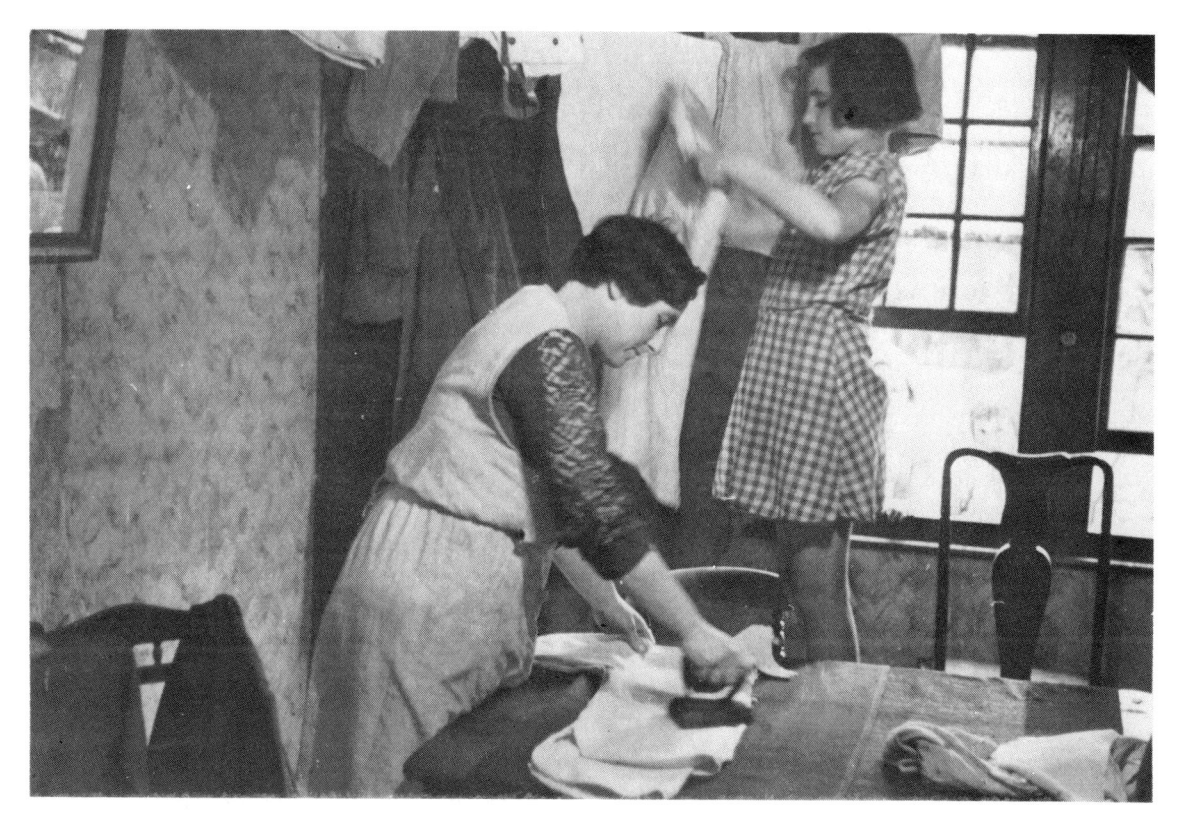

57 Life for a family on the dole between the wars was hard. This woman is doing the ironing with a "flat iron", heated on the stove. She uses the dining table with a blanket on top as an ironing board.

The Breakdown of Class Distinctions

The First World War accelerated changes in the structure of society which would otherwise only have come gradually. The class system, so much part of British life, did not vanish overnight, but inequalities in housing and living conditions began to grow less, and the working classes were less willing to accept their so-called "place" in society.

Men and women in the forces travelled, were educated in new skills, and met people whom they could never have known before the war. Women who had been domestic servants found better-paid alternative work in a factory. One girl like this said after the war:

I was in domestic service and hated every minute of it when war broke out, earning £2 a month working from 6.00am to 9.00pm. So when the need came for women war workers my chance came to 'out'.

For three hours less work each day, she could earn £20 a month, compared with £2 as a servant. Such girls did not go back into service after the war, and middle-class housewives employed daily maids instead, or did the housework themselves.

The conscription of women during the Second World War was even more comprehensive than in the First. Every woman between 16 and 49, unless exempt, could be directed into employment, with the result that all classes worked together at the factory bench or in the forces.

War was a great leveller for men as well as women. People had a feeling of shared experience — particularly noticeable during the Blitz in the Second World War, when communal life in air-raid shelters did much to improve neighbourliness. Evacuees also became

58 A First World War poster illustrating the changes in women's clothes because of the war.

accustomed to a different way of life, as did those who housed them. In both wars the restrictions on food, fuel, entertainment, travel and transport affected rich and poor alike.

In the nineteenth century a person's social class could be determined by his clothes. Today distinctions of this kind have almost vanished. The first changes took place during the First World War, when women were forced to wear shorter skirts and to cut their long hair for working in munitions factories. Between the wars short skirts and bobbed hair became symbols of women's emancipation. Clothing was rationed in the Second World

59 Second World War poster asking for women volunteers to help with the evacuation of children from towns which might be bombed, to new homes in the country. Many London children had never been in the country before.

War and women were encouraged to "Make Do and Mend". As an article in *The Observer* of 28 June 1942 recommended:

Women must expect to wear clothes now until the elbow wears out, but garments can be sent back to be refashioned as before.

Home dressmakers found ways round the regulations and made clothes from curtains, parachute silk and even blackout material, bleached and dyed. "Utility" clothing, which had been introduced in 1941, was praised at the time in *Vogue* magazine because

all women have the equal chance to buy beautifully designed clothes suitable to their lives and income. It is a revolutionary scheme and a heartening thought. It is, in fact, an outstanding example of applied democracy.

After the war there was a reaction to wartime restrictions in dress but, soon, cheap, fashionable, washable clothing was being produced for women, which all could afford. Men back from the Services wore the standard "Demob Suit", issued when they signed off. By the 1960s the young of both sexes were to adopt the classless fashions of denim and jeans.

After the restrictions of the Second World War and the immediate post-war period, there was an upsurge in industry and prosperity in the 1950s and 60s. Wages increased, education improved, and many women worked, at least until they got married. In 1945 only 26% of houses in England and Wales were owner-occupied. By 1973 the number had risen to 53%. The proportion of houses rented from local authorities doubled, and those rented from private landlords dwindled. There was a general "levelling up" of housing standards. Furniture design had been influenced by "Utility" styling during the war and furniture was becoming simpler and less costly. Television introduced people to new life-styles and products. Where once the essentials of home life had been a fire, a table and chairs and a bed, now everyone's basic requirements also included a refrigerator, washing machine, television set, deepfreeze, tape recorder, record player, and, of course, a car.

8
A Woman's Place

Hearth and Home

Until the present century women have had few rights. Girls were restricted in education and in the choice of jobs. Daughters could not inherit property and women did not have the vote. There was certainly no equal pay.

60 "Warm Thoughts about Matrimony". A group of women discuss their chances at the end of the eighteenth century.

Girls were expected to marry, and single women were regarded as second-class citizens, usually destined to be companions or servants in someone else's household. A "home" was for a family, but the family unit was larger than it is today, often including grandparents as well as other relations.

Marriage was not a partnership between equals. Wives were their husbands' chattels. They could not own property independently and their husbands could beat them without fear of the law. A wife's dowry became her husband's on marriage. Women had little control over the size of their families, and divorce was almost impossible. Society considered that a wife's place was in the home and for "home", the word "kitchen" could be understood.

A wife's position in society was determined by her husband's job. In the Middle Ages wives of important landowners often had positions of responsibility, but only as stand-ins for their husbands. In the absence of her husband, such a woman might become manager of the estate and household. However respected these women were, it never affected society's definition of a woman's role. A thirteenth-century French treatise summed this up with the advice: "Women should not learn to read or write unless they are to be nuns."

In the Tudor period, the wife of the owner of a large estate had heavy responsibilities. She was expected to oversee all aspects of the household, including the dairy, the kitchen garden, brewing and bee-keeping, and also to act as family doctor. Several books were written about household management and cookery in the sixteenth century, indicating that some girls must have been able to read. Although a certain amount of learning in a woman was admired, the general opinion was expressed in a play by the Elizabethan playwright John Lyly, by a character who remarked to a girl: "A needle will become thy fingers better than a lute."

Wives of shop-owners and other tradesmen in the sixteenth and seventeenth centuries also led busy lives as partners in the family business. Their homes were generally in their place of work, and they could employ maids to help in either establishment. Many women took sole charge of the shop or tavern if they were widowed.

William Vaughan's book denouncing *The Monstrous Regiment of Women* was published, rather ironically, when Elizabeth I was on the throne. He wrote: "Let wives be subject to their husbands" and "endeavour to please them by all means". Perhaps this is one of the reasons why the Queen herself did not marry. Vaughan defined a woman's role as being to "oversee her household, and to bring up her children and servants in the fear of God". However, Elizabethan women must have had more freedom than their contemporaries on the Continent, as a visitor to England in 1575 thought it a "Paradise of Married Women", where wives had leisure to play cards and visit friends.

As a new, prosperous middle class grew up in the eighteenth and nineteenth centuries, who had made their money in farming or industry, husbands began to dislike the idea of their wives working at all, even in the home. Even in modest households, servants did the work and wives spent the day embroidering, letter-writing or visiting. A Swedish visitor to England in 1748 thought that wives had become very lazy, compared with those in his homeland.

They never take the trouble to bake, because there is a baker in every parish.... Nearly the same can be said about brewing. Weaving and spinning is also in most houses a more than rare thing, because their many manufacturers save them from the necessity of such.

In the nineteenth century there were still plenty of servants available, willing to work for low wages. Middle-class husbands did not want their wives to do housework, as having servants distinguished the family from their working-class contemporaries. It was equally improper for single and married women to work outside the home, unless forced to by poverty. Countless books of advice on household matters were written, often by clergymen, which brain-washed women into believing that their place was in the home. Typical of these was Henry Southgate's book on household management, called *Things a Lady Would Like to Know*, which opened with the sentiment: "A loving woman is an angel in the house", followed by a quotation from a Rev. C.J. Vaughan:

We do not think that woman will ever find her crown ... in quitting her privacy and usurping the functions of statesman, of orator, of professional workman. We incline to think that, in grasping at power, she will lose influence.

The sanctifying of home life was a peculiarly Victorian method of keeping women in their place. With little opportunity to do useful work inside or outside the home, many became bored and unhappy.

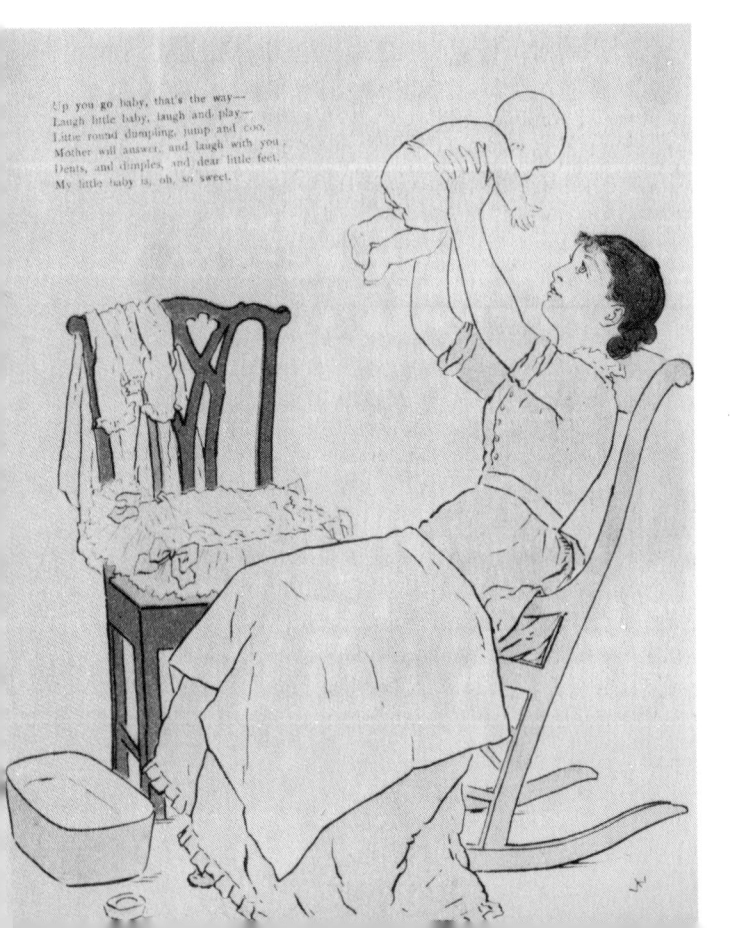

From early copies of the *Girl's Own Paper*, first published in 1880, it is clear that many women had become disenchanted with the domestic ideal. Girls wanted to do worthwhile jobs, at least until they got married. From the first, the paper gave advice on work and suggestions for finding and furnishing a place of one's own. At last, it was acknowledged that single women needed their own home as much as single men and married couples did. Much good advice was given about renting rooms, painting them and furnishing them cheaply.

Whereas most Victorians thought a perfect lady was someone who had never done a job of work in her life, by 1892 a *Girl's Own Paper* contributor was writing:

Too often ladies hide the fact that they have to work for their living, as if it were an everlasting disgrace and could never be forgotten. This is one of the old-fashioned ideas, which, it is to be hoped, a more enlightened age will wipe out.

The new job opportunities were still only suggested for single girls. Married women were expected to stay at home. Magazines suggested that instead of housework and cooking, which were done by servants, there were various crafts which a wife could learn, to beautify the home. These included making pictures out of shells, decorating fireplaces in summer with home-made paper flowers, doing embroidery with fish-scales, making brooches and wreaths from human hair, and decorating screens with cut-out paper — to name but a few. The crafts all took a great deal of time, but the Victorians loved to fill their rooms with ornaments of all kinds.

Men being away in the forces during the First World War gave women the opportunity to try their hands at a variety of jobs. They

61 Victorian writers believed that motherhood was a woman's supreme vocation. This illustration is from a typical book of the 1870s and '80s, called *Wee Babies*.

became accustomed to having a wage packet and gained new independence. It was difficult enough for anyone to get a job during the Depression, but after the Second World War everything changed. Many women had adjusted to having a job as well as coping with children, meals and housework. It was good to get back to normal after the war, but, as the authors of a post-war book of advice to couples, called *Living Together*, recognized:

> *Many [women] will ... feel that they are going back to prison, unless they have*

62 A "method of decorating a fireplace in summer", from *Cassells Household Guide*. Middle-class Victorian wives, who had servants to do the housework and cooking, had time to over-decorate their homes in ways like this.

63 Women protest about the lack of government nurseries for their children in 1942 to enable them to help in war work.

some life away from sinks and brooms and washtubs.

The post-war years have seen an enormous expansion in the number of married women in employment.

Working-Class Families

The poorer members of the population never had any choice about whether their wives worked or not. Until the twentieth century the wives of agricultural labourers worked side by side with their men in the fields, and children joined in, too, as soon as they were old enough. When they came home in the evening, wives had to find time to cook and look after the house in bad light, as electricity did not come to rural areas until well into the twentieth century. It is not surprising that little housework and washing was generally done. Country children seldom attended school during the harvest, only going to class in the winter when there was no work to be done on the land. Whole families were hired for a job, and a substitute had to be found if one of them was ill. Women received about half a man's wage for their work in the nineteenth century.

During the late eighteenth and nineteenth centuries some women found work in factories and mills, where their husbands might also be employed. They took their older children with them, but they were forced to leave their babies with child-minders, in squalid and unhygienic surroundings. Some women worked at home, as spinners, weavers or dressmakers, using the living room of their house as a workroom.

Women and Homes Today

Domestic life has changed completely in the last hundred years. One of the major causes is the new position of women in society. Today, women of every social class have the same educational and job opportunities as men. The principle of Equal Pay was established in 1970 and the Sex Discrimination Act of 1975 opened professions to women from which they were once barred. One result of this is that women do not necessarily rush into marriage. Another is that the majority of married women now work, at least until they have children. A third result is that wives may sometimes have better-paid jobs than their husbands.

Within marriage a wife has more legal protection than in Victorian days. Even if she does no outside job, it is recognized that she has the right to a proportion of the family home in case of divorce. The Domestic Violence Act gives protection to wives who are "battered" by their husbands — something which a Victorian husband could do with impunity. The Divorce Reform Act of 1971 has made the ending of a bad marriage much easier for a wife than it was in the past.

It is still difficult for wives with small children to work, but at least the Employment Protection Act of 1975 has guaranteed paid

64 A modern view on the roles of the sexes by cartoonist Mel Calman.

maternity leave to women who have worked for the same employer for more than two years.

Home life has changed because wives go out to work. In the first place, two incomes mean that a family can afford to buy new furniture and equipment, and go abroad for their holidays, as only the rich could afford to do before 1939. New household gadgets take the place of servants. A deep-freeze can be stocked up once a month from the supermarket, and so there is no need for endless shopping. Electric food processors grind meat and mix cakes. Instant packet soups and complete frozen meals can be dished up without much trouble. A dish-washing machine deals with the crockery. Clothes are sent to the laundry, put in the washing machine or taken to the laundrette. Cleaning equipment and new polishes take some of the labour out of housework. Even bedmaking becomes simple with fitted sheets and a duvet. Central heating is automatic and makes no dust.

However, although much of the hard labour had gone out of housework, the new gadgets were not always as quick as they seemed, and, at least up to the 1970s, women were still expected to do the chores, even if they had full-time jobs. Women in better-paid jobs often employed "au pair" girls to help with the house and children. These girls were the nearest modern equivalent to "live-in" servants of the past. The difference was that they came from abroad, with the principal purpose of learning the language — doing the housework coming a poor second. "Au pairs" were treated as members of the family and for this privilege worked long hours for little pay.

Partly as a result of the Women's Liberation Movement, founded in 1968, the nature of marriage is being redefined today, and rigid ideas about which are masculine and which are feminine roles are being reconsidered. A woman's place is no longer "in the home", any more than is a man's. Couples today work it out for themselves. Sometimes a man will even stay at home and look after the children for a time, and his wife will be the breadwinner. The couple themselves can make the choice and divide the jobs between them. Everyone is not the same, and some women will always prefer to stay at home to look after the house and family, just as there are some women who prefer to accept the status given to them through their husband's job, rather than earn the position in their own right.

Although the nature of marriage has changed today, a wedding is still a cause for celebration and friends give the couple presents, to help them set up their new home together.

Biographies

Mrs Beeton (1836-1865). Isabella Mary Beaton was trained as a pianist, but became known through her book *Household Management*, which was published in 1859 and much influenced middle-class eating habits.

William Harrison (1534—1593) was a geographer and historian at the time of Elizabeth I. He was educated at Westminster School and Oxford and became Chaplain to Lord Cobham, who gave him the rectorship of Radwinter in Essex. He helped to compile a history and description of England as it was during the reign of Elizabeth, which was published in the 1570s, and which gives vivid accounts of life at the time.

George Mitchell (1827—   ) worked until he was nineteen as a farm labourer in Montacute, Somerset, where he was born. He then became a marble mason and later had a prosperous business in London. He remained concerned with housing conditions for rural workers in Somerset, and was interviewed for the Royal Commission on Housing of the Working Classes in 1884. He published a book about his early life called *The Skeleton at the Plough* in 1874, showing how an agricultural worker lived in the early years of Queen Victoria's reign.

Tommy Morgan (1892—1971) was born in London's East End, off the Blackfriars Road. His childhood, which he described to Thea Thompson for her book, *An Edwardian Childhood*, was poor but happy. The Morgan family lived in one room, and were often thrown out by landlords for failing to pay the rent. Tommy's mother had thirteen children, but several died in infancy. Tommy Morgan's recollections are of a life of poverty and violence, but he was a survivor and lived to the age of seventy-nine.

Flora Thompson (1876—1947) was born at Juniper Hill, a village on the borders of Oxfordshire and Northamptonshire. In 1939 she published her autobiography, *Lark Rise*, which describes the life of her village in her youth, in about 1887. Two more volumes, *Over to Candleford* (1941) and *Candleford Green* (1943), followed, and all three books are now being published together under the title *Lark Rise to Candleford*. Her last book, *Still Glides the Stream*, was published a year after her death. It deals with her life in another village, as assistant to the local postmistress just before the First World War.

Parson Woodforde (1740—1803). James Woodforde was educated at Winchester and New College, Oxford. He was appointed vicar at Weston, Norfolk, while still a young man, and his five-volume *Diary of a Country Parson* records his happy life. He never married, but had a small circle of friends and parishioners who visited each other frequently and ate enormous meals together.

Glossary

bachelor chambers　a set of rooms in a large building, rented to a single man. At first, they were used in connection with the legal profession.
beetle　bat with a heavy head, once used for beating the washing clean.
black lead　polish containing graphite, used to clean old-fashioned iron fireplaces.
brazier　iron pan or basket containing lighted charcoal or coke, and used as a portable heater.
bureau　writing desk with drawers.
callers　another name for pedlars.
carpet sweeper　implement with revolving brushes which is hand-operated to sweep a carpet. It does not have the power of suction like a vacuum cleaner.
coachman　driver of a horse-drawn carriage of any kind.
Common Land　land belonging to the community: unenclosed wasteland in medieval period and up to the eighteenth century, with free right of pasturing.
consumer goods　goods (especially luxury items) used directly by ordinary people, not by manufacturers.
damp-proof course　layer of damp-proof material in a wall of a house, near the ground, to prevent damp rising from the ground.
dolly　special stick for stirring clothes when washing them.
dresser　kitchen sideboard with shelves above it, often used for displaying china. Sometimes built into an alcove beside the fire in the living room of old cottages.
drugget　coarse woven material used for floor or table covering. Also sack of woven material used to protect furniture from dust or sunlight.
estate　total land and buildings owned by an individual in one area.
feudal　describes the relationship between master and servant, based on land, where the farmer owes services and dues to his lord in return for permission to work the land.
fireback　iron sheet for back wall of fireplace, often ornamented.
firedogs　metal supports for burning wood in fireplace.
flagstones　flat slabs of paving stone, used indoors or out.
flock　special finish of finely chopped silk or wool, resembling velvet, and used on wallpaper from the mid-eighteenth century.
footman　uniformed servant who waits at table, at the door, or in the carriage of a wealthy family.
Grand Tour　a European tour on which sons from wealthy families were sent in the seventeenth and eighteenth centuries to complete their education.
Hall　large, central, public living room of a medieval home.
livery cupboard　small cupboard for keeping food overnight.
mansion　large house.

master of horse keeper of the stables in a wealthy household — now only used in connection with the Royal Family.

mortgage arrangement through which money is lent to the would-be purchaser of a property and the debt repaid over a period of years, during which time the property belongs to the creditor.

packman another name for pedlar.

Primus portable stove burning vaporized oil, used for cooking where no gas or electricity are laid on.

rates tax levied on home owners by local authorities, the amount according to the property owned, and used for local amenities such as schools, roads, sewage, waste disposal, water supply, etc.

retainer trusted servant.

rookeries crowded cluster of tall, slum buildings. Used in the Elizabethan period to refer to derelict town mansions filled with poor families.

settle bench with high back and storage space under the seat.

slum dwelling with overcrowded and squalid living conditions. Generally applied to buildings in a city rather than in the country.

suburb outlying area of a city.

tied cottage cottage "tied" to a particular job. Occupancy of the cottage is conditional on the occupier working for the cottage's owner.

truckle bed servant's or pupil's low, wheeled bed, which could be pushed out of the way, below the master's.

usher or "gentleman usher". Servant who acts as doorman, showing people of rank into a house.

whitster laundry maid.

Note on old money and measures

Money

Money was counted in pounds, shillings and pence (£-s-d). There were 240 old pence (d) in a pound, and 12 old pence (d) in a shilling (s). 20 shillings (written 20s or 20/-) made a pound.

Old Money	New Money
2.4d	1p
1s (1/-)	5p
2/6 (2s 6d)	25p
10s (10/-)	50p
1 guinea (£1-1s)	£1.05

Measurements

1 foot = 0·3 metre
3 feet (1 yard) = approx 1 metre

Books for Further Reading

Alison Adburgham,
Shopping in Style,
Thames & Hudson, 1979

Eleanor Allen,
Home Sweet Home,
A & C Black, 1979

Eleanor Allen,
Wash and Brush Up,
A & C Black, 1976

Pat Barr,
The Framing of the Female,
Kestrel Books, 1978

Ronald Blythe,
Akenfield,
Allen Lane, Penguin Press, 1969

Rose M. Bradley,
The English Housewife in the 17th and 18th Centuries,
Edward Arnold, 1912

Jenni Calder,
The Victorian Home,
Batsford, 1977

Norah Lofts,
Domestic Life in England,
Weidenfeld & Nicolson, 1976

Arthur Marwick,
Women at War,
Fontana Paperbacks, 1977

Thea Thompson,
An Edwardian Childhood

Flora Thompson,
Lark Rise to Candleford,
Penguin, 1939

James Woodforde,
The Diary of a Country Parson,
Oxford, 1968

Look also at old copies of *Girl's Own Paper*, *Cassells Household Guide* and other periodicals.

Museums

Folk Museums and Museums of Rural Life
throughout the country, including:

Abbey Barn Museum of Rural Life, Glastonbury
Geffrye Museum, London
Science Museum, London
Castle Museum, York
Museum of English Rural Life, Reading
West Yorkshire Folk Museum, Halifax
Winchester City Museum, Winchester
Wolvesnewton Folk Museum, Nr Chepstow

Index

The numbers in **bold** type refer to the figure numbers of the illustrations

advertising 52, 53; **13, 26, 36, 37, 38, 40, 53, 54, 58, 59**

baths 22, 23, 49, 55; **18, 19**
building societies 17

children 7, 9, 10, 46, 47, 49, 55, 58, 61, 62, 63, 64; **5, 41, 44, 46, 49, 57, 59, 61, 63**
cleaning 36–39; **35, 36, 37, 38, 48**
  spring cleaning 39; **36**
clothes 58–59; **58**
cooking 43–45; **44**
  dutch oven 43
  electricity 44; **38**
  gas 21, 44
  haybox 45
  kitchen range 44; **16, 44**
  open fire 20, 43; **14, 27**
  Primus 44

Defoe, Daniel 10
Dickens, Charles 10, 51

electricity 10, 18, 21, 27, 44, 45, 49, 64; **24, 38, 41**
Evelyn, John 6

food
  preservation and storage 43
  rationing 54, 55; **55**
  utensils 45; **43, 45**
  (*see also* cooking, meals)
furniture 29–35, 59; **32**
  beds 13, 29, 31, 68; **30**
  chairs 30, 33; **5, 14, 15, 28, 34, 46, 47, 60, 61**
  chest **29**
  sideboard 30; **31, 34**
  table 30; **5, 23, 34, 46, 47**

gas 10, 21, 27, 44
governesses 7

Harrison, William 19, 27, 31
heating 19–23
  central heating 21, 56
  coal 20, 21; **15, 16, 32**
  electricity 21; **24, 38**
  gas 21
  wood 19; **5, 14, 27**
housing 11–18
  back-to-back 15; **11**
  castles 13, 30, 31
  Chambers 15; **10**
  cottages 11, 12, 19, 25, 27, 29, 31, 32, 36, 43, 49, 68; **6, 7**
  council 18; **56**
  flats 15, 22, 45, 56; **56**
  mansions 13, 14, 31; **8**
  prefabricated **56**
  semi-detached 56
  slums 14, 33, 46, 55, 68; **11, 21**
  suburbs 17, 56, 68; **13**
  terraced 11, 12

interior decoration 27–28; **25, 26, 62**

kitchen, *see* cooking

laundry 39–40; **39, 40, 41, 57**
lighting 25–27
  candles 26, 27; **22**
  electric 19, 27; **24**
  gas 21, 27
  oil 26; **23**

marriage 5–9, 60–65; **1, 2, 3, 4, 54**

meals 9, 13, 46–47, 65; **5, 46**
(*see also* cooking, food)
Mitchell, George 12, 25, 46
Morgan, Tommy 14, 21, 33, 41

pedlars 50; **50**

radio 10; **33**

servants 47–49, 57, 61, 65, 68; **4, 18, 19, 35, 36, 39, 40, 47, 48, 49**
shops 50–51; **31, 51, 52**
suburbs, *see* housing

television 10
Thompson, Flora 7, 12, 21, 22, 23, 25, 32, 41, 42, 46, 50, 51

unemployment 56

wallpaper, *see* interior decoration
wartime conditions 54, 56, 57, 62, 63; **55, 58, 59**
water 22, 23
(*see also* baths)
  stand-pipe **17**
  well **7**
WCs 24–25; **21**
Welfare State 56
Woodforde, Parson 5, 20, 43, 47, 50

71